STARTING IN TAEKWONDO

Training for Competition
&
Self-Defense

Joe Fox & Art Michaels

Sterling Publishing Co., Inc.
New York

With profound thanks and appreciation . . .

- To my wife, Cathy, my son, Sam, and my daughter, Jamie, for their patience and encouragement while I wrote and photographed this book.

- To my teacher and co-author, Master Joe Fox, who continues to teach me a wealth of Taekwondo.

- To Master John Null and Sabumnim (instructor) Brian Hinman, who also taught me much Taekwondo.

- To Master Anthony Grafton and instructors Don Brink, Janelle Silvers, Kristin Davin, John Bolden, Shawn Sanders, Tim Manning, and all the instructors and students at the Harrisburg Institute of Taekwondo for being my training partners and letting me photograph their demonstrating the techniques in this book.

- To Dr. Mark Mascari for informative interviews and medical opinions in several chapters.

- To Sherry and Ty Sterling, owners of Gold's Gym, Harrisburg, PA, for use of the facility to photograph Chapter 4.

- To Robert K. Fujimura, former Executive Director, United States Taekwondo Union, for reviewing some material and providing photographs.

- To John Corcoran, former editor of *Inside Taekwondo,* and Marian K. Castinado, former editor of *Dojang* and editor of *World of Martial Arts,* for their encouragement and advice.

Art Michaels

Library of Congress Cataloging-in-Publication Data

Fox, Joe.
    Starting in taekwondo : training for competition & self-defense / Joe Fox and Art Michaels.
        p. cm.
    Includes index.
    ISBN 0-8069-6104-X
    1. Tae kwon do. I. Michaels, Art. II. Title.
    GV1114.9.F69 1997
    796.'153–dc20

96-35886
CIP

Edited and
QuarkXPress Design
by Rodman Pilgrim
Neumann

10 9 8 7 6 5 4 3 2 1

First paperback edition published in 1998 by
Sterling Publishing Company, Inc.
387 Park Avenue South, New York, N.Y. 10016
© 1997 by Joe Fox and Art Michaels
Distributed in Canada by Sterling Publishing
℅ Canadian Manda Group, One Atlantic Avenue, Suite 105
Toronto, Ontario, Canada M6K 3E7
Distributed in Great Britain and Europe by Cassell PLC
Wellington House, 125 Strand, London WC2R 0BB, England
Distributed in Australia by Capricorn Link (Australia) Pty Ltd.
P.O. Box 6651, Baulkham Hills, Business Centre, NSW 2153, Australia
Manufactured in the United States of America
All rights reserved

Sterling ISBN 0-8069-6104-X Trade
                0-8069-6109-0 Paper

Disclaimer

Contents

Preface

HOW MANY TIMES have you asked yourself these questions:

- Will the Taekwondo techniques I'm learning work in self-defense and in competition?
- Which techniques are the most useful?
- How do I apply all that I'm learning?

When I began Taekwondo training, I asked these same questions that most students ask. To find the answers, I trained eagerly, of course, and I consulted my teachers. I also searched libraries, book stores, book publishers' catalogs, martial arts supply company catalogs, and martial-arts magazines. I found various bits and pieces of answers from all of these places, but nowhere was I able to find a comprehensive source that explained which Taekwondo skills were the most practical and how to apply these new skills.

This book is the training supplement I wish I'd found. *Starting in Taekwondo* is a thorough explanation of Taekwondo's most practical basic techniques with illustrated specifics on how to apply the techniques in competition, self-defense, and daily training. I've also made sure to explain in this book how to make the most of your Taekwondo training.

During my early years of Taekwondo practice, I also began to discover precious training secrets that martial artists learn only from experience:

- How to avoid major and repeated injuries, yet not sacrifice my training regimen.
- How to recover as quickly as possible from injuries.
- How to balance training to achieve the maximum progress, while getting adequate rest.

Of course, uncovering the answers to these questions is the main challenge of the ranks below black belt. And no matter how eagerly I trained, only through experience and continuous training did I begin to learn these lessons. Even as I progressed, the answers to these questions changed gradually from time to time. In addition, I learned that the answers that suit one student might be different from another student's experience.

More than specific answers, I wanted to be pointed in the right direction to make the most of my training. My teachers showed me this path. This book explains some of those "road signs" to help you find your own path.

Art Michaels

1. Warm-ups, Cooldown & Stretching

TAEKWONDO IS NOTED for its kicking, so stretching the legs is extremely important. In Taekwondo training you want to try to attain your maximum flexibility, and stretching lets you do that. Stretching also decreases the risk of injury.

Everyone's degree of flexibility is different. Factors that affect flexibility include a person's age, body build, current physical condition, and capability. Regardless of how flexible you are, don't stretch specifically to be more flexible, especially if you're a beginner, and don't compete with anyone when it comes to stretching. We're all different, so an appropriate stretch for you might be too much of a stretch for another student and not enough of a stretch for someone else.

Stretching is, however, very much an individual pursuit. Stretch regularly and properly only for you.

Stretching is vital in Taekwondo training because it increases the blood flow to a muscle. A muscle's smaller blood vessels dilate during stretching to let more blood flow into the muscle. Stretching enhances circulation, and it allows the muscle cells to take in more nutrients and carry away waste more efficiently.

When you stretch a muscle properly, you squeeze the muscle tissue and flatten it, as if you were stretching a rubber band. You also lengthen the muscle, which enhances its elastic quality.

Stretching creates a memory in the muscles. When you finish stretching, the muscle goes back to its "normal" state. Over time, stretching teaches the muscles to remain elongated.

In Taekwondo training you want to try to attain your maximum flexibility, and stretching lets you do that. Stretching also decreases the risk of injury.

Warm-up, Cooldown

To decrease the risk of straining muscles and injuring joints during stretching, there are warm-up and cooldown. Warming up isn't stretching with the muscles "cold." Most people are "warmed up" for stretching when they start to sweat from light activity. That usually takes about five minutes of walking briskly, jogging, using a stationary bike, jumping rope or performing calisthenics—doing something to break a sweat. This warm-up increases the core body temperature by a degree or so.

Warm-up and cooldown stretching begin after the body is warm. Most warm-up and cooldown stretching should be done from the ground, either sitting or lying down. Standing while stretching can increase the risk of injury to the lower back because of the bending and twisting you perform.

Proper warm-up and cooldown stretching means feeling mild discomfort during the stretch. A dull ache is an appropriate amount of discomfort during correct warm-up and cooldown stretching. Sharper pain, burning pain or piercing pain is a danger signal that means you're stretching too far, you're not stretching properly, or you have sustained an injury.

The following seven stretches provide an adequate warm-up for Taekwondo training.

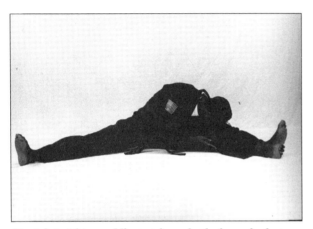

Stretch 1. *This straddle stretch works the lower back, inner thighs, and hamstrings.*

Stretch 1. This straddle stretch works the lower back, inner thighs, and hamstrings. Begin sitting on the floor with the legs open comfortably. Keep the lower back straight with the shoulders back. Draw the chest and stomach forward. Concentrate on proper body position. Stretch from the hips and lower torso—straight ahead and then down each leg. Exhale as you go into the stretch, and relax.

A common mistake with this stretch is making the back round and craning the head and neck forward.

Stretch 2. A similar stretch begins with sitting on the floor, both legs together and straight. Lean forward, drawing the stomach and chest toward your knees. Keep the head up and look straight ahead. Grab your ankles or calves. Don't pull, forcing the stretch. Use your muscles to stretch, and relax into the stretch. Remember to exhale into the stretch.

Stretch 3. Sitting up straight on the floor with both legs together and straight, bend the right knee and tuck the right sole against the left inner thigh. Reach out with both hands down the left leg. This stretch works the hamstrings, shoulder muscles, and torso.

Now reverse the stretch, tucking the left sole against the right inner thigh. Reach out with both hands down the right leg.

Stretch 2. *Keep the head up and look straight ahead. Grab your ankles or calves. Don't pull, forcing the stretch. Use your muscles to stretch, and relax into the stretch. Remember to exhale into the stretch.*

Stretch 3. *This stretch works the hamstrings, shoulder muscles, and torso.*

Stretch 4. Sitting up straight on the floor with both legs together and straight, bend the right knee and bring the right leg over the left leg, placing the right foot flat on the floor. Draw the right knee into your chest and twist your body to the right. This stretch works the buttocks area. Reverse the legs, stretching both sides.

Stretch 5. This stretch works the inner thigh muscles. From a sitting position draw the heels in as close as you can toward the buttocks. Keep the legs open and the knees as close to the floor as you can. Hold the toes and gently lean down each leg.

Stretch 4 works the buttocks area. Reverse the legs, stretching both sides.

Stretch 5 (left and center) works the inner thigh muscles. Remember to keep the lower back straight, stretching from the lower torso and the hips. Gently press the forearms on each leg above the knees, flattening the knees to the floor.

Remember to keep the lower back straight, stretching from the lower torso and the hips. Gently press the forearms on each leg above the knees, flattening the knees to the floor.

Stretch 6. This stretch is useful for isolating and gently stretching the inner thigh muscles. Sit with your legs parallel to a wall. Bring your legs up the wall, placing your buttocks about six to 12 inches from the wall and your back flat on the floor. Touch the wall with your heels. Let the weight of your legs gently open the stretch.

Stretch 6. This stretch is useful for isolating and gently stretching the inner thigh muscles. Let the weight of your legs gently open the stretch.

Stretch 7. The primary upper body area to stretch is the lower back. It is the key to overall flexibility. If the lower back is tight, kicks aren't going to be high even though the hamstrings and buttocks are flexible.

To stretch the lower back and hamstrings differently from the floor stretches, stand with the feet pointing straight ahead about a shoulder width apart. Bend the knees slightly as you bend over. Keep the knees bent in an inch or two. Don't lock the knees. Let your arms hang down toward the floor, or for support hold on to a chair or other support. You can also place your hands just above the knees for support during this stretch. As you stretch the lower back and hamstrings, gently and slowly turn your torso slightly to both sides.

To recover from this stretch, bend the knees even more and point the feet out. This flexes the quadriceps, taking the strain off the lower back as you recover to an erect position.

When you complete the warm-up and these stretches, you're ready for progressively more strenuous, Taekwondo-specific exercises and stretches.

Increasing Flexibility

The biggest difference between stretching to warm up and your stretching to increase flexibility is that to increase flexibility you stay in the stretch longer and take the stretch a little farther. Another way to increase flexibility is to fatigue the muscle with isometric exercises in a stretch, or by holding the stretch longer than usual. In this way, a muscle taken to failure is less likely to tear. It'll relax a little more and you'll get a deeper stretch.

Weight training ties into increasing flexibility by performing a high number of repetitions with light weight. Loose muscles need adequate support, which means increasing the strength of the

Stretch 7 works the lower back, the primary upper body area to stretch. The lower back is the key to overall flexibility. If the lower back is tight, kicks aren't going to be high even though the hamstrings and buttocks are flexible.

To decrease the risk *of straining muscles and injuring joints during stretching, always be sure to warm up and cool down. Warming up isn't stretching with the muscles "cold." Most people are "warmed up" for stretching when they start to sweat from light activity. That usually takes about five minutes of walking briskly, jogging, using a stationary bike, jumping rope, or performing calisthenics—doing something to break a sweat.*

Why Increase Flexibility?

In Taekwondo training, increasing flexibility has a practical purpose that isn't always obvious. This purpose isn't the general health benefits of stretching or the value of warming up and cooling down.

"Increasing flexibility" actually means increasing the range of motion in a joint. Appropriate stretching and strengthening accomplishes that. When you increase the range of motion in the hip joints, for example, you can kick higher and more effectively. However, increasing the range of motion in a joint also means generating more speed as you perform techniques. Speed is the main ingredient in power. The faster you can execute a technique, the more power you can generate.

Consider a pebble. Pick it up and toss it at someone, and it won't hurt him. Throw it as hard as you can, increasing its speed, and it causes more damage. Now propel that pebble at a much faster speed in a slingshot, and it can cause considerable damage.

Thus, increasing flexibility increases a joint's range of motion. More range of motion lets you generate more speed in the technique. More speed means more power in kicks, punches, and blocks

muscles around the joints as you increase flexibility. Strengthening muscles while increasing flexibility also helps prevent joint injuries. Tension stretching (isometric stretches)—that is, performing kicks very slowly—also strengthens and stretches the leg muscles.

The repetitiveness of strengthening exercises causes muscles to hypertrophy—the muscle fiber thickness grows. As the muscle thickens from strengthening and as its elasticity and length increase from regular stretching, the muscle can simply do more. You can then meet the same stretching or kicking demand that previously might have injured the muscle.

When to Stretch

Perform relaxed stretching every day, once in the morning when you rise and before you retire—each with a warm-up. Sessions should last 10 to 15 minutes.

Ideally, arrive at Taekwondo class about 15 minutes early so that you can warm up and stretch. Of course, that's not always possible. That's why most classes begin with warm-up drills and stretching.

Stretch to increase flexibility three times a week. However, don't stretch to increase flexibility and then begin hard Taekwondo kicking drills. During the forceful snapping motions of kicking drills there is too much of a chance that you can pull a muscle or hurt a joint.

Right after Taekwondo class is a good time to stretch to increase flexibility. Your muscles are most likely adequately warm then. After stretching to increase flexibility, remember to cool down—perform light exercises followed by the same stretches you performed to warm up. Remember: to cool down, perform all the steps of warming up but in reverse order.

Two-Person Stretching

Two people working together on stretching can achieve better results than working alone on a machine. With one person holding your leg up, for instance, you can prac-

Consider lifting a heavy object–something everybody's done. At the point when you exert yourself the most, you grunt, or make some kind of noise. That's essentially a *kihap*–bringing forth all your strength from your lower abdomen.

The mistake that some students make with the *kihap* is that they yell from the throat. That is just a noise. It may startle an opponent, but it doesn't enhance power.

A proper *kihap* should be brought forth from the *danjun*–that part of the lower abdomen from which you draw your power. Breathing exercises help you summon this power.

First Moving Concentration Exercise

Moving concentration exercises help you to direct your power in different directions through your breathing. The idea is to enable an 85-pound person to direct every pound into a weapon toward a target–or a 50-pound child, or even a 250-pound adult. Just because someone appears to be "big," it doesn't mean that person is powerful and strong. The key is learning to direct one's power. That's also why someone who weighs only 85 pounds isn't necessarily frail.

The first moving concentration exercise focuses the power upward and releases it downward. Start in junbi position.

Cross your arms in front of your chest as if you were preparing to execute a high block.

The *kihap* is actually your taking all of the breath and power that you have built, blowing it out, and directing it to a certain weapon and target. The technique that you use with a *kihap* is meant to stop your opponent. With the *kihap*, a technique is more forceful than when it is ordinarily performed. The *kihap* helps you to direct your power to whichever part of the body is the weapon.

Tense your entire body, and with slow, tensed movement raise the "boulder."

Step out into a horse stance and at the same time kihap *and thrust the arms outward to the sides and down, as if you were preparing to lift a huge boulder (arrows). Open the fingers widely. Control your breathing during the exercise.*

Think of directing and focusing power as if you had a 10-inch round, solid-metal cylinder and a nail. The nail penetrates a board readily because it's more focused and concentrated in a particular spot. You can pound the cylinder all day and it won't go into the same board.

The first moving concentration exercise focuses the power upward and releases it downward. Start in *junbi* (ready) position. Cross your arms in front of your chest as if you were preparing to execute a high block. Step out into a horse stance (refer to Part Two, Chapter 5) and at the same time *kihap* and thrust your arms outward to the sides and down, as if you were preparing to lift a huge boulder. Open the fingers widely. Bend the knees.

Control your breathing during the exercise. Tense your entire body, and with slow, tensed movement raise the boulder. When your hands are overhead, release the power downward and

Focal Point

During all these exercises, it's important to touch the thumbs to the index and middle fingers. Let the pinkies and ring fingers rest on or near the palms. This gives you a focal point toward which you can direct your power. Until you develop the ability to direct internal energy to a specific part of the body—a weapon—it's difficult just to hold your finger out and "make power" there. Lightly touching the index and middle fingers with the thumbs helps you direct your power to the area you can feel with the touch.

backward between your legs, as if you were throwing the imaginary boulder between your legs behind you. Release with a burst of total exhalation.

Bring your hands to an overhead position.

Release the power downward and backward between the legs, as if you were throwing the boulder behind you between your legs. Release with a burst of total exhalation.

Directing your power upward applies to any upward movement—an upper cut, high block, or high front kick, for example.

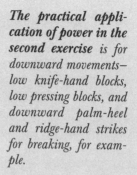

The practical appli-cation of power in the second exercise is for downward movements— low knife-hand blocks, low pressing blocks, and downward palm-heel and ridge-hand strikes for breaking, for exam-ple.

The second moving concentration exer-cise directs your po-wer downward and releases it off to the sides. It begins as the first exercise, in junbi position.

Then cross the arms and step out into a horse stance with a kihap.

Second Moving Concentration Exercise

This exercise directs your power downward and re-leases it off to the sides.

It begins as did the first one, crossing your arms and stepping out into a horse stance with a *kihap*. This time, draw your arms close to the rib cage. Imagine two huge wooden stakes on each side of your body that you are trying to drive into the ground with your hands. Remember to control your breathing through-out this exercise. Bend your knees. As your body goes downward, use your whole body to force the two imaginary stakes into the ground. When you are unable to lower yourself any farther, release out to the sides. Remember to release with a burst of total exha-lation.

This time, draw the arms close to the rib cage. Imagine two huge wooden stakes on each side of your body that you're trying to drive into the ground with your hands. Remember to tense your body and control your breathing throughout this exercise.

Bend your knees. As your body goes downward, use your whole body to force the two imaginary stakes into the ground.

When you can't lower yourself any farther, release out to the sides. Remem-ber to release with a burst of total exha-lation.

The third exercise helps you concentrate your power across the plane of the body (arrow), as in some ridge-hand strikes, round-house kicks, some knife-hand strikes, and inside forearm blocks, for example.

***This exercise** fo-cuses your power inward. Start just as you did in the first two exercises—in* junbi *position.*

***Then cross your arms,** kihap, and step out into a horse stance.*

Third Moving Concentration Exercise

This exercise focuses your power inward. Start as you did in the first two exercises—arms crossed, *kihap*, and stepping out into a horse stance.

This time, keep your arms straight, palms facing backward and hands bent at the wrist. Imagine your arms chained to a wall behind you, and you are pulling the chains in toward your chest. Just short of touching your chest, release outward in front of your body. Remember to control your breathing during this exercise and release with a burst of total exhalation.

***This time** keep the arms straight, palms facing backward and hands bent at the wrist. Imagine your arms chained to a wall behind you, and you're pulling the chains in toward your chest. Remember to tense your whole body and control your breathing during this exercise.*

***Bring the arms** to a position just short of touching your chest.*

***Release outward** in front of your body. Remember to control the breathing and release with a burst of total exhalation.*

***Continue** tensing your body and controlling your breathing, and bring the arms closer together.*

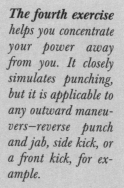

The fourth exercise helps you concentrate your power away from you. It closely simulates punching, but it is applicable to any outward maneuvers—reverse punch and jab, side kick, or a front kick, for example.

The fourth *exercise is a little different from the other three. Its movements are more dynamic, and it's not as slow and concentrated. Start as before, in* junbi *position.*

Cross your arms, *kihap, and step out into a horse stance.*

Fourth Moving Concentration Exercise

This exercise is a little different from the other three. Its movements are more dynamic—not as slow and concentrated. Start as before—arms crossed, *kihap,* and stepping out into a horse stance. This time, draw the open hands to your chest, near your solar plexus, with the palms facing downward.

Remember to touch each hand's thumb to the index and middle fingers. As a training partner or your instructor counts, direct your power away from you, directly in front of you, as if you were throwing small objects—quickly and forcefully turning the hands over and pointing the fingers outward. Quickly bring the hands back to the starting position each time. Let the count be rhythmic. Get into your own rhythm of controlling your breathing and letting out a *kihap* at the moment you release forward on each count.

As a training partner *or your instructor counts, direct your power away from you, directly in front of you, as if you were tossing something—quickly and forcefully turning the hands over and pointing the fingers outward. Quickly bring the hands back to the starting position each time. Let the count be rhythmic. Get into your own rhythm of controlling your breathing and letting out a* kihap *at the moment you release forward on each count.*

This time *draw the open hands to your chest, near your solar plexus, with the palms facing downward. Remember to touch each hand's thumb to the index and middle fingers.*

Practicing and Applications

These exercises can be very draining if you perform them at 100-percent strength. For this reason, the best time to practice them is at the end of class, after class, or at home.

Understanding the application of these exercises and how they tie in with proper breathing is vital. In all your training activities, and the moving concentration exercises, controlling your breathing and *kihap* work together the same way.

In competition, controlling the breathing and using *kihap* correctly help you muster your power, but controlling your breathing also lets you disguise your fatigue. An opponent sees only your rhythmic breathing. Determining whether an opponent is tired can be difficult without observing the obvious sign of panting with the mouth open.

In forms practice, remember that you're defending yourself against multiple attackers. To maximize your power, practice inhaling as you prepare to strike or block, and exhale as you perform each technique. You must also learn to inhale and exhale in spurts, when you block and strike together, and when you perform several blocking and striking techniques quickly in one burst.

Examine all your forms, and consider when to breathe slowly, inhaling with each preparation and exhaling with each block or strike, and also when faster movements require you to breathe faster or in spurts.

Are you already testing the effectiveness of your techniques by practicing breaking boards (*see* Chapter 20)? The idea of controlling your breathing to maximize your power is the same for breaking as it is in other applications. At the

Kihap & Taking Blows & Falls

In addition to its role as a focuser of power, *kihap* is also a cleanser. You need it most when you fall or take a blow.

When a person says that he "had the wind knocked out of him," he actually had it stuck inside him. The diaphragm goes into spasm and doesn't move. It can't push air out then. When a person starts to draw air in again, there's no room because the lungs are already filled. If you *kihap* when you're hit or when you fall, that air comes out, and when you do inhale again, there's room for more air. The *kihap* lets you begin breathing again normally much faster.

An attacker on the street or a competitor might see the panic in your eyes, knowing that he's stunned you, or that he's "knocked the wind out of you." An alert opponent, in competition or on the street, won't give you the opportunity to recover. For this reason, learning to breathe properly and learning the correct use of *kihap* is essential.

point of striking, exhale and *kihap*. Anyone can perform some amount of succesful breaking with sheer force. Beyond a certain point, however, force alone does not work. Technique, knowing the proper way to strike, conditioning, and breathing correctly let you summon all your focus and power to a small target. For this reason, when you go beyond your physical strength in breaking, breathing properly is the key to success.

3. How to Use the Training Hall Mirror

THE TRAINING HALL MIRROR is an excellent training aid that can help you improve almost all aspects of your technique. It takes some practice, though, to learn how to make the best use of the mirror and to know when not to use the mirror.

If you're a beginner, don't underestimate the value of the mirror because it might intimidate you. You might see yourself in the mirror, knowing that others might be watching, so you're likely to think the mirror is a distraction, not a training aid. You need to learn that in class you focus on your own technique in the mirror. You also look in the mirror at more advanced students if you forget a technique, or if you need to see how an advanced student executes a technique. After a while you realize that all the students are focusing for the most part on themselves.

If you line up at the back of the class, use the mirror to check more advanced students' technique and confirm that you are performing it correctly.

Your teacher might tell you that you're making a mistake with a technique, but to you it feels right. Seeing the error or refinement in the mirror helps you change the technique quickly.

You probably have noticed that during class warm-up and kicking drills your teacher sometimes stands at the back of the training area. The teacher can't always see all the students perform techniques, but from the back of the training area the teacher uses the mirror to see who might need help with techniques.

You and the other students probably face the mirror during these drills. In this way most students can see themselves in the mirror. Move a little to one side if you can't see yourself during class exercises and drills, or move so that you can see a more advanced student whose technique you can imitate. You can occasionally check out your technique in this way.

Class mirrors are most often at the front and back of the training area. You might be distracted by mirrors on the sides of the class, because you and other students look often to see yourselves and others. If the choice is yours, train with the mirror either in front of you or behind you.

The training hall mirror is an excellent training aid that can help you improve almost all aspects of your technique. It takes some practice, nevertheless, to learn how to make the best use of the mirror and to know when not to use the it. If you line up at the back of the class, use the mirror to check more advanced students' technique and confirm that you are performing it correctly.

Stances

Stances are some of the first techniques taught in Taekwondo, but if you're a beginner they can be a continual source of difficulty. The mirror can help you master stances. In a front stance, for instance, you have to square the hips and shoulders, bend the front knee, keep the back leg straight, maintain the correct width and distance between the feet, and not cock the body. A front stance sounds easy but, for beginners, managing all these parts of a front stance is difficult.

Your teacher checks you now and then, but the instructor can't help you all the time. Performing strong, technically correct stances comes with checking yourself in a mirror. You learn the correct way by seeing yourself in the mirror and repeatedly confirming the correct stance, so you can make many adjustments on your own, between the times your teacher works with you.

Your teacher might tell you that you're making a mistake with a technique, but to you it feels right. Seeing the error or refinement in the mirror helps you change the technique quickly.

When you perform a front stance, or any stance, in a mirror, you may still feel terribly awkward. When you can see yourself in the mirror, however, you can confirm that you're performing the stance correctly.

Check your stances often in a mirror, because each stance has so many parts. All the parts must be done correctly. What feels awkward at first becomes comfortable as you check and recheck each stance's parts in the mirror.

Your teacher checks you now and then, but the instructor can't help you all the time. Performing strong, technically correct stances comes with checking yourself in a mirror. You learn the correct way by seeing yourself there and repeatedly confirming the correct stance, so you can make many adjustments on your own,

Even advanced students sometimes forget their foundations, so advanced students should also periodically check their stances in a mirror. Executing techniques powerfully comes primarily from performing strong, balanced, technically correct stances. That's why checking stances in a mirror is important for all students.

between the times your teacher works with you. Perform stances from different angles and check yourself in the mirror from different angles. All you have to do is glance at the mirror from whichever position you take.

Even advanced students sometimes forget their foundations, so they also should periodically check their stances in a mirror. Executing techniques powerfully comes primarily from performing strong, balanced, technically correct stances. That's why checking stances in a mirror is important for all students.

Kicking Techniques

When you practice jumping techniques, for instance, you might think that you are chambering–raising the knee to the chest with the leg bent–the non-kicking leg because both legs are off the ground. But your non-kicking leg actually might not be chambered. When you watch yourself execute a jumping kick in front of a mirror, as you extend the kick, you can see if the non-kicking leg is chambered. Then, continuing to practice in front of the mirror, you can improve the technique by remembering to tuck in the non-kicking leg.

Work on keeping your hands and arms close to your body during these kicks. Do not let them swing away from your body. Sometimes your arms will tend to swing out as you perform the technique, even though you think you're keeping your arms near your body. The mirror can help you correct this problem, too.

Lining Up in Class

Look straight ahead when you line up in class in front of the mirror. Imagine an opponent or an attacker directly in front of you. When you train alone, or in an informal class, stop immediately during different parts of the technique and check your technique in the mirror. Correct any errors and try not to make the same mistakes. Continue practicing this way until you see in the mirror that you're executing the technique correctly, or that you've corrected an error. Then check your technique in the mirror only occasionally.

The mirror helps you improve techniques in the same way as a heavy bag helps. When you execute a spinning back kick, for example, you kick at the right time because, as you spin, you

---

Warning

Some students become dependent on the training hall mirror. If they can't observe themselves in the mirror, they are not able to perform techniques correctly.

The mirror can help any student learn new skills and improve technique. But after you've corrected a technique or honed it, don't practice in front of the mirror. Just use the mirror occasionally. Some students come to think of the mirror as a target, and without the mirror they can't execute techniques correctly. If you work out in front of a mirror often, move away from the mirror now and then.

Your teacher may direct the class to turn away from the mirror occasionally during warm-up drills. Your teacher may have observed that for some students the mirror is becoming a distraction or it's becoming the focus of too much attention.

---

see the target in the mirror. You become the target, and it's either in front of you or it isn't. In most Taekwondo schools, not all students can use the bag at the same time, so you use the mirror to practice on yourself as the target. The mirror helps you ensure that you execute the spinning kick in the right direction at the right time.

Similarly, beginners can use the mirror to confirm that they chamber and re-chamber each kick. You might think you're chambering kicks properly, but practicing in front of a mirror can show you whether or not you're actually positioning the leg correctly.

Beyond Technique

Observing correct form is only the beginning in using the training hall mirror. You observe the body and body motion in the mirror. Practicing in front of a mirror can help you learn to use your peripheral vision–an asset in self-defense and in competition.

Blindfold Test

Mirror training has a flip side: blindfolded training. Blindfolded training helps you improve your forms, sparring, basic techniques, step sparring, grappling—anything. In the mirror you learn the correct imagery—grasping each technique's purpose. You have to visualize the purpose of every technique. When you have cultivated this skill and you are performing techniques correctly, then your teacher might blindfold you.

Training in darkness is quite a different world. Blindfold training helps you and your teacher confirm that the feel you have of performing a technique actually corresponds to your doing it properly.

Consider placement of kicks. When you are blindfolded, if you direct a side kick to the abdomen, and you can't see your foot or the target but you have visualized the technique in your mind correctly, then the technique is probably "yours." This confirms the naturalness of the technique, and the likelihood increases that the kick will be effective for you in competition and in self-defense.

Try simply facing a part of the training area different from what you are used to and perform a form. You might be surprised that this small change can confuse you. Putting on a blindfold also obscures this reliance on orientation. The key is to learn to perform techniques smoothly in any direction. Blindfolded technique helps you and your teacher ensure that your focus is correct.

For competition, you can also observe which parts of the body move first when you perform kicks and punches. For the most part, if you first have to move the shoulder, elbow, hip, or knee to execute a technique, then everyone else probably has to move that body part first to execute a punch or kick. This idea applies equally to competition and to self-defense.

You have the advantage when you see an attack coming, because then you can observe the body part that is moving to understand what must move first. By observing yourself and others in the mirror, you learn what happens first in an attack.

For this reason, let the mirror help you learn to focus on the upper part of the opponent's torso. From this view you can see all the different body parts. You won't be fooled when someone tries to distract you with the eyes, because you're not looking at the opponent's eyes. This kind of mirror training helps you become a better fighter and a better defender.

4. Basic Weight Room Workout

IF YOU WANT TO GET SERIOUS about Taekwondo, and if you want to enhance your strength, flexibility, and stamina, you should expand your training with weight room workouts. Combining your Taekwondo class training with regular visits to the weight room can help you punch, block, and kick harder and faster.

You might believe that weight room workouts will diminish your speed and flexibility. The misconception is that if you lift weights, you become tight and slow. The opposite is true. This weight-lifting program can complement your Taekwondo training. It's geared toward increasing flexibility and speed if you work out in the weight room correctly.

Before lifting, try biking, running, jumping rope, performing light calisthenics, or working on a stepper machine to break into a bit of a sweat and get the blood flowing. Then go into light stretching. After a weight room workout, perform the same kind of cooldown–breaking into a light sweat and stretching. Chapter 1 includes more details of warming up, stretching, and cooling down.

This weight room program includes developing the major muscle groups of the chest, back, legs, and abdominals, as well as the minor muscle groups of the biceps, triceps, shoulders, and forearms. Of course, you need each of these muscle groups to perform Taekwondo techniques.

Before lifting, *try biking, running, jumping rope, performing light calisthenics, or working on a stepper machine to break into a bit of a sweat and get the blood flowing.*

Back

Start with the back muscles. A beginning program includes front and back lat pull-downs. "Lat" refers to the name of the large muscles of the middle back: *latissimus dorsi*. These muscles gives the torso its "V" shape. Front pull-downs isolate the middle and lower lats. Back pull-downs work the upper lats.

Also perform low rows, which hit the middle and upper lats, and dumbbell rows, to work all the upper back muscles.

Start with three lifts for each muscle group, and as your strength, stamina, and speed increase then you can add more challenging exercises to your regimen.

A pec deck isolates the inner chest muscles.

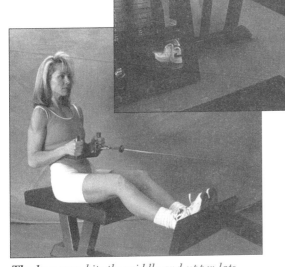

Incline bench presses *with barbells work the upper chest muscles.*

Front lat pull-downs *isolate the middle and lower* latissimus dorsi *muscles of the back.*

Chest

Try three exercises initially for working the chest muscles. Isolating the chest muscles is important because punching and blocking work primarily the upper and inner chest. Work all the chest muscles to achieve balance and develop the body evenly. However, hit the upper and inner chest muscles harder than other chest areas to enhance punching and blocking power.

Start the chest workout with incline bench presses using barbells. This exercise works the upper chest. Flies, or working a pec (pectoral) deck, isolate the inner chest, and a dip machine helps hit the upper and front chest.

Back lat pull-downs *work the* upper *latissimus* dorsi *muscles of the back.*

The low row *hits the middle and upper lats.*

Leg curls hit the hamstrings.

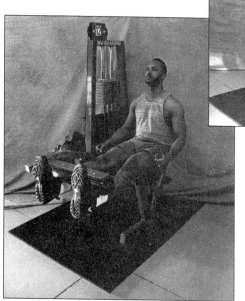

Leg extensions work the quadriceps.

Legs

In Taekwondo you kick a lot, and at advanced levels you perform a fair amount of jumping. That's why you have to work the quadriceps, hamstrings, and calves, along with the inner thigh and hip flexors.

For the quads, start with leg extensions. Then hit the hamstrings with leg curls.

Work the calves with three exercises: seated calves, donkey calves, and standing calves. In a seated calf, you sit and push up weights placed on the knees. In a donkey calf, you stand bent over and push up weights on your back. In a standing calf, you place pads on your shoulders and push weights up.

Standing calves work the calf muscles. These calf exercises are vital to developing jumping ability and fast, powerful blitzes.

Seated calves also work the calves.

The quads and calves are important for jumping, and the hamstrings come into play with front kicks, ax kicks, and crescent kicks. The calves are also important for executing takeoffs, and for the competitor, the blitz. You need to work the calves to develop that fast, powerful sprinting motion that a successful blitzing technique requires.

You could start a program for the inner thigh and hip flexor muscles on a cable crossover machine, but this might not be wise if you're a beginner. As the other leg muscles become used to working out with weights, you can introduce cable crossover exercises for the inner thighs and hips after about one or two months.

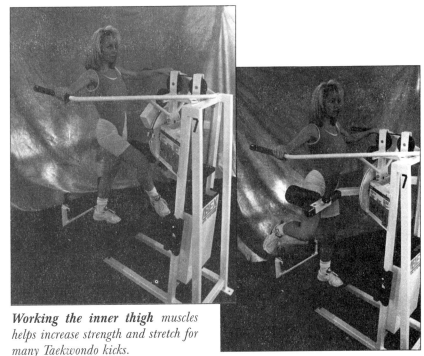

Working the inner thigh muscles helps increase strength and stretch for many Taekwondo kicks.

Hitting the hip flexors also helps increase strength and flexibility for Taekwondo kicks.

Breathing

Breathing correctly during weight room workouts is just as important as breathing properly in Taekwondo class. When you execute a kick, block, or punch, you exhale. Exhaling summons more power into the technique, and it also helps you focus power to the weapon. Breathing this way is the same as when weight-lifting. When you lift, exhaling focuses your power. To get the most from your workout, breathe properly.

Don't hold your breath during these exercises and exhale at the last moment. As you bring the weight back to the starting position, inhale. As you end the lift, your inhaling is at its peak. Breathe rhythmically this way when you lift.

If you breathe incorrectly, you starve the muscles of the oxygen they require. You'll become tired sooner than you would if you were breathing properly. When you work a muscle that doesn't get enough oxygen, the muscle produces lactic acid. A burning sensation in the muscle is an indication that the amount of lactic acid in the muscle is increasing. When that begins, the muscle stops performing. A muscle stops working when you take it to failure, and it builds lactic acid; but failure occurs sooner when you breathe incorrectly than when you breathe correctly.

For more details on breathing correctly, see Chapter 2.

The bent-over raise works the back part of the shoulder and the trapezius muscle.

The front raise isolates the front part of the shoulder muscles.

Shoulders, Biceps, Triceps

Hit the shoulders next. The shoulder muscles are important to punching and blocking, and it's important to develop each part of the shoulder. That's why you should start with four lifts for the shoulders.

The military press—lifting barbells or dumbbells up and behind the neck—works the back part of the shoulder and the trapezius muscle. Using dumbbells in front raises exercises the front part of the shoulder. Side raises work the sides of the shoulders, and bent-over raises exercise the back part of the shoulder and the traps again.

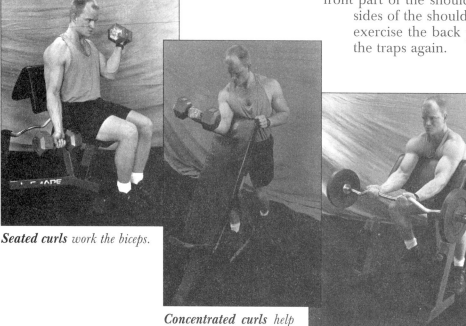

Seated curls work the biceps.

Concentrated curls help isolate the biceps.

Preacher curls isolate the biceps even more.

Kickbacks *work the triceps.*

Triceps extensions *also work the triceps.*

Next, use two or three lifts to work the biceps. The biceps aren't as important as other muscle groups for Taekwondo students. Working the biceps helps a lot in pulling, for the grappling arts.

To work the biceps, start with standing or seated barbell or dumbbell curls. Then perform concentrated curls–placing the forearm on the knee while seated to isolate the biceps. You can also perform concentrated curls by placing the arm on an incline support. "Preacher" curls isolate the biceps even more. In a preacher curl you lean over a pad while seated. With the other curls it's possible to "cheat" a little–other muscles help in the exercise. With the preacher curl you can't cheat. It's a direct isolation of the biceps.

The triceps and shoulder muscles are two of the least used muscles in everyday activity, but they are very important to punching power. Start with push-downs–grabbing a small bar and pushing straight down to work the triceps. Next, go to triceps extensions with barbells or a machine. In this exercise, you sit in an inclined position and push the weight upward.

The third triceps exercise is a kickback. Place the arm at about a 90-degree angle and push a weight backward, twisting the arm.

Warm-up & Cooldown Reminders

Do warm-up stretching. This increases the blood flow to the muscles and prepares them for more strenuous activity. Cooldown stretching helps contracted muscles "remember" to stay long and stretched. Stretching also enhances the circulation, letting the muscle cells take in more nutrients and carry away waste more efficiently.

Stretch gently. This kind of stretching is not geared toward increasing flexibility. The goal of warm-up and cooldown stretching is to feel a slight discomfort. If you feel sharp pain–or burning, piercing pain–ease the stretch.

Always be careful to warm up before you stretch. Generally speaking, this means breaking into a sweat.

Stretch the muscles twice, with a moment between stretches. Let each stretch last 30 seconds to about a minute to two.

Crunches work the abdominal muscles. *Keep the hands across the chest and don't press or jerk upward from the neck.*

Abdominals

The abdominals are the most important muscles that you can develop. You summon your power from the lower abdominal area. In addition, the better condition your abs are in, the less likely you'll develop lower back problems.

Develop the abs with a variety of crunches–tensing the abdomen, but *not* doing a sit-up–and machine work. For starters, lie flat, knees bent, with the arms across the chest. From this position, lift the shoulders for crunches, without using any weights. A second crunch requires pulling your knees and shoulders together to hit the lower abs. As you progress, put weights on the chest to create more resistance. At a more advanced level, work the abs on a "crunch" machine.

Forearms

Work the forearms primarily for the grappling arts. However, knife-hand strikes and rising blocks require strong forearms to be their most effective, and if you have well-developed forearms you lessen the chances of injury when you perform these techniques. Wrist curls and squeezing a tennis ball develop the hands, wrists, and forearms.

You work the forearms, wrists, and hands in all the other lifts because you're gripping, pulling, and pushing, but you can still isolate the forearms with these and other isometric and tension exercises.

To perform a wrist curl, wind a rope around a bar or dowel, alternately twisting the bar with the hands and fingers. As your strength increases, you can add more weight to the bottom of the rope.

Sets, Repetitions

For all these exercises, start with low weights. The starting weight depends on your current level of fitness. Nevertheless, you should choose a weight that lets you perform 12 to 15 repetitions of each exercise in three sets. By the time you reach the third set, you should feel very fatigued. If you choose a weight that's too heavy to begin with, you'll stray from good technique just to get the weight up. Then you diminish the effectiveness of the exercise and increase the risk of injury.

Barbells can help *work the forearms. Exercise by moving the wrists up and down, while squeezing the bar.*

Take It to Failure

The purpose of these routines is to take the muscles to failure. This means that by the time you reach the end of the third set, you simply cannot move the weight. The idea in taking a muscle to failure is that you tear down the muscle with the exercises so that the muscle will rebuild stronger.

Remember that "taking a muscle to failure" and simply "challenging a muscle" are actually quite different. Challenging tones and firms a weakened muscle, but taking a muscle to failure breaks it down. When you rest, the muscle then renews itself and becomes stronger. You can increase your strength a little by working out until you tire, but you won't gain as much as you would if you took the muscle to failure.

This kind of weight training also increases endurance, and endurance is certainly a major part of Taekwondo training. You might not have to throw a lot of punches, kicks, and blocks in a self-defense situation, but sport Taekwondo and regular training call for much repetition, so muscle endurance is a must. If strength is your only asset and you can punch, kick, and block only a few times before you tire, that may not serve you.

Increase the repetitions and lower the weight to develop endurance. That means performing 12 to 15 repetitions in each set instead of eight to 10 or fewer.

Full Range of Motion

Focus on moving through your full range of motion in all these lifts. If you use the full range of motion in the exercises and stretch diligently before and after each weight room session, you can increase your flexibility along with your strength and stamina.

Scheduling Workouts

Rest is very important, so don't exercise the same muscle group two days in a row. Some people's schedules might cause them to work every muscle group in one session. They don't achieve the best results because after you work one major muscle group and you try to work another major muscle group, by the time you get to the second muscle group you're too fatigued to work it the way you should to get the best results.

Instead, exercise one muscle group each day, or work two different muscle groups per workout. For instance, in one session exercise the back and biceps, then in the next session hit the chest and triceps, and then the shoulders and legs. Remember to let the muscles rest at least a day after weight training. For more details on resting properly, see Chapter 22.

If you go to Taekwondo class and weight-train the same day, try to perform these activities at least two or three hours apart. You prevent injuries best when you rest properly between workouts. Many people lift on alternate days three days a week and go to Taekwondo class the other three days.

Don't stop Taekwondo training for six months or so simply to get stronger by lifting. You have to keep doing both so that your flexibility and technique don't suffer. Stopping your Taekwondo training simply to get stronger is when you're actually more likely to tighten up and slow down.

Do you practice breaking? If you train at breaking, after you've been lifting for a while you'll notice an increase in what you can do. A certain amount of breaking is physical, and to progress, of course, you must focus and prepare mentally. Nevertheless, your lifting will let you increase your physical ability to break, and that's more of an objective measurement than simply noting how you feel.

After a while you'll also notice an increase in the power at the end of your punching, kicking, and blocking in sparring, forms or when you practice alone. You'll also notice an increase in your stamina.

Remember—if you want to increase your strength, speed, and flexibility, lift weights *and* train. Let both kinds of exercise work for you.

Push-ups *with the hands held directly beneath the shoulders (left) work the triceps. Push-ups with the hands farther apart (right) work the chest muscles.*

The back stance is the position from which most Tae-kwondo practitioners fight. From junbi, *execute a left-side back stance first by turning the right foot 90 degrees to the right, pivoting on the ball of the foot, not the heel. Bring the left foot straight ahead about one shoulder width. Bend both knees and push them outward. Keep the back straight. About 60 to 70 percent of your body weight should be on the back leg.*

To execute a horse stance from junbi, *move the left leg about two shoulder widths to the left, keeping the back straight. Push the knees outward, and keep both feet pointed straight ahead. The horse stance is not a practical stance for fighting because body position in this stance limits the techniques you can execute. However, the horse stance is primarily a training stance, useful in strengthening the inner thigh muscles, quadriceps, and back and stomach muscles. Practicing the horse stance will also make the other stances stronger.*

Back Stance

The back stance is the position from which most Taekwondo practitioners fight. From a *junbi* ready position, execute a left-side back stance first by turning the right foot 90 degrees to the right, pivoting on the ball of the foot, not the heel. Bring the left foot straight ahead about one shoulder width. Bend both knees and push them outward. Keep the back straight. About 60 to 70 percent of your body weight should be on the back leg.

Check for proper positioning of the back leg. When you look down at your right leg, you should look in a straight line from your shoulder to your hip and to your heel.

Common mistakes with this stance are that students place the left foot (front foot) too far to the right, making the stance narrow, or placing the left foot too far to the left, exposing too much of the body and making it difficult to execute techniques. Students also extend the left foot too far forward.

The key to maintaining a strong, effective back stance is that you want to be solid, but not too solid. You don't want to be "glued" to the ground so that you need an extra movement before you can execute a technique with either foot. Extra movement, such as shifting your weight or taking another step, telegraphs to an attacker or a competitor that you're about to execute a technique.

Horse Stance

The horse stance is not a practical stance for fighting, because body position in this stance limits the techniques you can execute. However, the horse stance is primarily a training stance, useful in strengthening the inner thigh muscles, quadriceps, and back and stomach muscles. Practicing the horse stance also makes other stances stronger.

To execute a horse stance from *junbi*, move the left leg about two shoulder widths to the left, while keeping the back straight. Push the knees outward, and keep both feet pointed straight ahead.

A common mistake with the horse stance is bending the knees inward, which creates a weak stance and an unbalanced body position.

Drills

Stance drills help you develop strength, flexibility, and balance, as well as your ability to move and execute techniques while in the stances.

Initially, you practice stances by putting the hands on the hips and stepping forward into right-side and left-side stances. When you can maintain the stance, practice moving drills—still with the hands on the hips. The goal in executing moving drills is to maintain the stance with good body positioning, weight distribution, and balance.

The next step is to achieve the same goals while moving backward in stances. Finally, practice turning while in a variety of stances.

Two-person drills are also beneficial. Two students face each other. One executes controlled kicks and punches as the other applies blocking techniques. Both students maintain good posi-

Stance drills let you develop strength, flexibility, and balance, as well as the ability to move and execute techniques while in stances. In this exercise, the attacker (right) would advance with punches in front stances while the defender (left) would block, stepping backward in back stances. Drills like these progress in difficulty of techniques.

tions in a variety of stances. Students can apply a variety of blocks and strikes.

This drill is beneficial because executing stances alone twnds to become easy after sufficient practice. But when someone pressures you with a technique, and you have to apply a block while also maintaining the stance, then executing your basic stance can at times become troublesome again. Drilling in this way helps you overcome this sort of difficulty.

The ability to execute stances in stationary positions, to move forward and backward, and to turn carries over directly into forms practice. The chances increase that when you practice forms with this foundation in traditional stances, you will better understand the movements in each form, have a greater sense of balance, and understand better how to control the body.

6. Front Snap Kick

THE FRONT SNAP KICK is one of Taekwondo's most basic and effective techniques. The front snap kick's weapon is the ball of the foot. If you target the groin, the instep can be the weapon. Some people who lack the flexibility to turn the toes back often use the heel as a weapon. The knee, groin, stomach, solar plexus, and chin are the primary targets for the front snap kick.

There are two common ways to perform a front snap kick. The kick is most often thrown out very quickly and then retracted quickly. It is also performed with more of a thrusting motion than a snap. You commit completely to the thrusting front kick because you drive your foot through the target.

The thrusting front kick is a weapon used mostly in full-contact competition. The momentum of performing the thrusting kick takes you forward. Recovering from this kick is more difficult because getting back into a balanced, defended position requires more effort than what you would need if you snapped out the kick and recovered quickly.

The front snap kick is one of Taekwondo's most basic and effective techniques. The front snap kick's weapon is the ball of the foot.

Basic Execution

In Taekwondo training, the front snap kick is often the first kick taught. Nevertheless, always execute this kick carefully. There's always room for improving technique to make this kick increasingly quick and powerful.

From a fighting stance with the right leg back, turn the hips toward the front—that is, square your body to an imaginary attacker—and raise the kicking leg into chamber. This means bringing the right knee to your chest. Chambering a front snap kick is important. Chambering gives this kick, and most others, power, and raising the knee to the chest helps protect the lower abdomen and groin before you execute the kick.

The front snap kick begins in a fighting stance.

From a fighting stance *with the left leg back, turn the hips toward the front—that is, square your body to an imaginary attacker.*

The chamber is also a block as you square off your body to your opponent.

From the chambered position, fire the kick forward, lifting the toes up and backward as you kick with the ball of the foot. Pointing the foot slightly downward and pulling back the toes exposes the ball of the foot and lets you extend the kick a little farther. Bring the leg back into chamber and place the kicking leg at the starting position.

You rotate the hips a little to execute a driving front kick. The more hip you turn into the kick, the more driving force you can muster. A snap kick to an attacker's knee needs little hip turning because the kick is meant to be fast and whip-like. A front kick to the solar plexus or stomach needs more hip turning because you want more driving force with this kick. If kick with your left foot, for example, you'd turn your hips to the right as you execute the kick.

Don't rotate the hips forward on this kick. Chances are, rotating the hips forward means stretching the hip muscles beyond their capability—putting you off balance and rendering the kick awkward and ineffective.

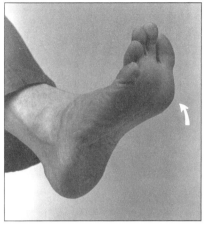

The weapon of the front snap kick *is most often the ball of the foot (arrow). Remember to hold the toes drawn backward throughout the kick.*

Remember to perform each movement in executing this kick, no matter how fast you learn to perform it.

Place the kicking leg *at the starting position.*

Bring the leg back *into chamber.*

From the chambered position, fire the kick forward, *lifting the toes up and backward as you kick with the ball of the foot. Pointing the foot slightly downward and pulling back the toes exposes the ball of the foot and lets you extend the kick a little farther.*

Raise the kicking leg into chamber. *This means bringing the left knee to your chest. Remember to keep the guard up.*

Practicing front snap kicks with a kicking shield is useful because it helps you increase power. As well working with a kicking shield will help you remember to pull your toes back.

Walking around the training area on the balls of your feet (arrow) is another useful way to learn to control the muscles around the toes. The ideal skill is to be able to pull the toes back and expose the ball of the foot as you execute a front snap kick.

Jump Front-Snap Kick

Jumping allows you to execute a front kick more forcefully than when keeping a foot on the ground. You can execute this technique almost straight up, attacking upward into the jaw, or you can perform this kick straight out.

There are two ways to execute a jump front-snap kick. You can attempt to get a reaction from an opponent by stepping forward first with your lead leg, say, the right leg. Then as the opponent blocks, you jump, lifting off the ground on your right leg. Kick with the left foot over the block. You can also perform a jump front-snap kick jumping straight up from both legs and kicking in one motion.

Jumping straight up and kicking in one motion requires more speed than the first move of stepping forward, especially when you face a seasoned fighter. If you kick too slowly, an opponent can jam you or fire off another kick or punch before you can execute the jump kick.

In one kind of jump front-snap kick, you attempt to get a reaction from an opponent by stepping forward first with your lead leg, say, the left leg. Start in a fighting stance.

Step forward with your left leg, as if you were walking up a step.

As your opponent blocks, you jump, lifting off the ground on your right leg. Kick with the right foot over the block.

You can also perform a jump front-snap kick jumping straight up from both legs and kicking in one motion. Start in a fighting stance.

Jump straight up and kick with the rear leg in one motion. You could also kick instead with the front leg.

The stepping jump front-snap kick becomes both a block and a decoy. When you lift the non-kicking leg and an opponent reacts, usually attempting to jam you as you kick, your chambered knee creates a little distance so that you can kick with the other leg. The opponent might be too close for you to throw a front snap kick, but with the chambered leg you can still fire off a side kick or a crescent kick.

Double Kicks

Double front-snap kicks are also useful. The first kick can be a decoy, like the jumping kick with a step. As with any double kick, mix your targets so that your opponent can't readily anticipate where you'll place the kicks. Work them high–low, low–high, and in other similar combinations. The second kick in a double kick should have more power and driving force than the first. Use the first kick as a feign. To execute this double kick, draw the kicking leg back into chamber after the first kick and fire it out again.

Kicking once, touching the floor, and then quickly kicking again is another kind of double kick. Use this kind of double front kick to lure your opponent closer to you. The second kick is the one you want to execute more powerfully.

Both double front kicks are designed to make your opponent move–to elicit a reaction. The opponent's movement and where you see the opening let you know where to aim the second kick.

Practicing front snap kicks with a kicking shield is useful because it helps you increase power. Working with a kicking shield also helps you remember to pull the toes back. Walking around the training area on the balls of your feet is another useful way to develop control with the toes as you execute a front snap kick. The ideal skill is to learn to control the muscles around the toes so you can pull the toes back and expose the ball of the foot.

A kicking shield is forgiving–another benefit of working with this training aid as you learn the front snap kick. If you don't pull the toes back properly, a kicking shield will "remind you gently" without your incurring a serious injury. A heavy bag is much less forgiving, so after you've developed control with the toes, work with a heavy bag.

Beyond the Basics

Twisting the hips and bringing the leg high into chamber are the important elements in the front snap kick beyond learning the basic mechanics of the kick. Quickly turning the hips squarely and quickly chambering the kick are vital to being able to launch this kick against an experienced competitor. An experienced fighter can see this kick coming without that speed, and every time you try to throw it, you might never be able to execute it fully.

Even the best fighters telegraph their techniques a little, so executing this kick with maximum speed is essential.

Self-Defense

The front snap kick is one of the few traditional Taekwondo kicks that can be practical in self-defense. You need only a minimum amount of training to learn to use this kick effectively, especially a kick to the knee. Executing a front snap kick also requires only a small amount of flexibility and balance, and controlling the toes isn't a big consideration if you're wearing shoes. While wearing shoes, point the toes and strike the attacker's knee with the point of the shoe.

Defenders telegraph this kick the least, so it's vital in self-defense training. Defending against a quick strike to the knee is also difficult.

Defending Against a Front Kick

Turning the hips too slowly before you bring the kicking leg into chamber is the most obvious signal that you're preparing to execute a front snap kick. When you see an opponent turn and chamber too slowly, jam the kick.

A thrusting front-leg side kick is a practical way to jam an opponent's front snap kick. Place your side kick below the knee as the opponent tries to chamber the leg. Of course, after unbalancing the opponent this way, follow immediately with combinations of hand and foot techniques.

Blocking and trapping is another way to defend against a front snap kick, especially in a self-defense situation. Suppose an attacker attempted a left-leg front snap kick. Evade by moving to your left, getting out of the way of the kick. Deflect the kick with your right hand. Trap the kicking leg with your left hand, reaching underneath the attacker's outstretched left leg. Step inside, putting your left leg behind the attacker's right leg. Upsetting the attacker this way opens his chin, nose, or solar plexus to your attack. You can then send the attacker to the ground. Finish with a groin strike.

Blocking and trapping is one way to defend against a front snap kick, especially in a self-defense situation. Suppose an attacker attempted a right-leg front snap kick. Evade by moving to your right, getting out of the way of the kick. Deflect the kick with your left hand.

Trap the kicking leg with your left hand, reaching underneath the attacker's outstretched left leg.

Step inside, putting your right leg behind the attacker's left leg. Upsetting the attacker this way opens his chin, nose, or solar plexus to your attack. You can then send the attacker to the ground.

7. Side Kick

BASIC TAEKWONDO TECHNIQUES can be surprisingly effective. The side kick is one such basic technique, and in many competitive and self-defense situations, it can be decisive. The side kick, a Taekwondo trademark, can work no matter how flexible—or inflexible—you are.

However, some Taekwondo students aren't flexible. To compensate for lack of flexibility when they execute a side kick, they bend the torso low and raise the leg as high as they can. Leaning downward lessens the kick's power.

On the other hand, some Taekwondo students are so flexible that they don't hone their side kick technique as they should, because with little effort they can shoot their legs high.

Basic Taekwondo techniques can be surprisingly effective. The side kick is one such basic technique, and in many competitive and self-defense situations it can be decisive. The side kick, a Taekwondo trademark, can work no matter how flexible—or inflexible—you are.

Both kinds of students—very flexible ones and inflexible ones—should divide executing the side kick into steps that focus on positioning the body, chambering the leg, and foot placement. This exercise can help any student develop an effective side kick, whether the student comfortably kicks low, mid-level, or high. Snap and speed are the keys to executing a powerful, effective side kick, but if you perform the kick incorrectly at any height, it won't be as effective as it could be.

"Concentrated Kicking"

Breaking down the side kick, or any kick, into its component parts and executing each part very slowly is called "concentrated kicking." This drill is one of the best ways to learn and continue to improve your side kick. The concentrated kicking exercise for the side kick includes five stages that divide the kick into slow-moving parts.

Start in a fighting stance with the right leg back. Raise the kicking leg—in this case, the right leg—into a snap kick chamber. This first part turns the hips squarely to the target. Next, rotate the hips to a side position and keep the leg in this side kick chamber. At this point, the kicking foot's blade should be turned slightly downward in a knife-like position with the toes raised. Now extend the kick. The kicking foot's heel should be in a straight line with the hips and shoulders. This position lets you put your full body weight into the kick, maximizing your kick's power. Next, re-chamber the kick and, finally, put the leg down, returning to the fighting stance.

Repeating this slow drill is more beneficial than firing fast side kicks all the time. Concentrated kicking strengthens and stretches all

Breaking down the side kick, or any kick, into its component parts and executing each part very slowly is called "concentrated kicking." This drill is one of the best ways to learn and continue to improve your side kick. Use a chair to help you maintain balance.

Your partner can also help you maintain your balance while you perform a side kick's steps very slowly. Such concentrated kicking strengthens and stretches all of the muscles used to execute the side kick.

the muscles used to execute the side kick, and it helps you keep your balance as you kick. During concentrated kicking exercises, you learn to keep your balance as you perform each step slowly. When you execute a side kick quickly, keeping your balance becomes easier.

Performing all the side kick's steps is vital, so concentrated kicking helps you include all the steps naturally as you increase its execution to full speed. With sufficient practice, you don't have to think about all the steps—they'll be there because of your concentrated kicking practice.

To execute a side kick, start in a fighting stance with the right leg back.

Turn the hips square toward the opponent.

Raise the kicking leg—in this case, the right leg—into a snap kick chamber.

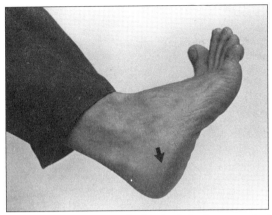

The side kick weapon is the blade of the foot near the heel (arrow).

When you execute a side kick, remember to strike with the blade of the foot near the heel. Don't strike with the flat part of the heel. The difference between using the flat part of the heel and the blade of the foot near the heel is like the difference between slapping a target and punching it with a closed fist. Striking with the blade of the foot lets you bring your full power into the kick.

As you perform a side kick, open the hips by pointing the foot of the support leg, or "plant foot," in the opposite direction of the kick. If you are very flexible, you might be able to perform a side kick without turning the support foot this way. Still, most people need to open the hips to create as much power as they can, and turning the plant foot in the opposite direction of the kick lets them do so.

Guard Up

When you perform any kick, it's important to keep the guard up—that is, keep the elbows close to the body, guarding the ribs, and hold the hands near the face, guarding the head. If an opponent or an attacker blocks your side kick, a counter will surely follow right away. If you let your arms flail as you kick, and if you lower your guard when you kick, your face, head, and body are exposed and defending against the counter is difficult.

Rotate the hips to a side position and keep the leg in this side kick chamber. At this point, the kicking foot's blade should be turned slightly downward in a knife-like position with the toes raised.

Now extend the kick. The kicking foot's heel should be in a straight line with the hips and shoulders. This position lets you put your full body weight into the kick, maximizing your kick's power. Re-chamber the kick, and put the leg down, returning to the fighting stance.

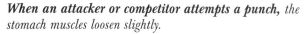

When an attacker or competitor attempts a punch, *the stomach muscles loosen slightly.*

You may have been taught to extend your arms when you execute a side kick, as if you were maintaining your balance on a balance beam. It's best to learn to keep the guard up while you kick. When you practice performing a side kick with the guard up and in, you develop balance in this position. If you let the arms flail when you kick–to stay balanced when you begin to hold the guard up and kick–you'll be unbalanced.

Learn right from the beginning to hold your guard up as you kick. As you learn to kick higher and perform more complicated kicks and combinations, you can keep your balance without letting the arms fly outward or dropping the guard. The height of your kicks will increase, and you'll maintain the kick's effectiveness and power as your flexibility and strength increase. The height, speed, effectiveness, and power of your side kick can't grow by forcing the kick up and using your arms to keep from falling.

You can develop a strong side kick by working with fellow students, with a heavy bag, and with the training hall mirror. Bag training helps you increase kicking power. You can perform side kicks at full power when you kick a bag. This suggests how strong your side kick is. Knowing what your side kick can actually do increases your confidence.

Catch the attacker with a side kick in the stomach *at this moment, and it will be easier to stop the attack or score a point .*

You learn distancing by training with a heavy bag and with partners. Kick too close and you jam the kick. If you chamber incorrectly, you can't strike the target effectively. Use a mirror to confirm that your kicking form is correct, and repeat the correct form as you practice.

Street Application

The higher you kick, the less power you have, unless you're one of the few Taekwondo practitioners who is very flexible, and the more open you become to counterattacks. In addition, environmental factors are important considerations in self-defense. Are you standing on gravel, snow, water, ice, stones, or grass? Are you on a flat surface or on an incline? Depending on what you're standing on and where you are, you might attempt a high side kick and slip.

In self-defense situations, the side kick is used most effectively on targets from the ribs downward, depending on how much danger you believe you're in. If you believe you must seriously incapacitate an attacker, target the leg just above the knee.

You can also disable an attacker with a side kick to the ribs. Kicking the ribs shows why snapping out the kick, chambering, and striking with the blade of the foot near the heel are essential. You're taking advantage of the attacker's forward motion and firing the side kick right below the ninth rib–the solar plexus. This hard kick, when properly thrown, forces the diaphragm upward, knocking the wind out of an attacker. The impact to the diaphragm makes it momentarily difficult to breathe.

When an attacker tries a front snap kick, a side kick to the stomach is a practical defense. When the attacker attempts the snap kick, the body twists forward. Driving a side kick into the attacker's stomach maximizes your side kick's effectiveness by using the attacker's forward momentum.

When an attacker attempts a punch or kick, the stomach muscles loosen slightly. Catch the attacker with a side kick in the stomach at this moment, and stopping the attack or scoring a point will be easier.

You can disable an attacker *with a side kick to the ribs. Suppose someone lunges at you with a punch. Kicking the ribs shows why snapping out the kick, chambering, and striking with the blade of the foot near the heel are essential. You're taking advantage of the attacker's forward motion and firing the side kick right below the ninth rib–the solar plexus. This hard kick, when properly thrown, forces the diaphragm upward, knocking the wind out of an attacker. The impact to the diaphragm makes it momentarily difficult for him to breathe.*

Sport Application

Applying the side kick in competition is the same as using it for self-defense, except that you don't kick below the waist and you throw side kicks with greater control.

The front-leg side kick is the primary side kick weapon in competition. A rear-leg side kick requires more motion and positioning to execute, so it's difficult not to telegraph this kick. For this reason, the rear-leg kick can be useful if you hurt an opponent and the opponent has lost most of the ability to defend himself.

The front-leg side kick is useful after you've drawn the opponent in toward you through a variety of tactics. For instance, you could lift an arm to expose the ribs, or you could fake a backfist. Both these ploys suggest to your opponent that your defense has an opening, or that you have a readable habit or pattern to your fighting. They draw your opponent in, at which point you execute a front-leg side kick to score.

A front-leg side kick can also be used to keep an opponent away. To accomplish this, you use the front-leg side kick as a boxer uses a jab. You keep sticking it repeatedly. This tactic lets you get a feel of what your opponent is doing and what his capabilities are. You also watch for patterns in his defense.

Remember that the side kick can be very effective both in self-defense and in competition. Dissect the technique and practice its parts slowly. Turn this Taekwondo trademark into one of your most effective weapons.

8. Roundhouse Kick

THE TAEKWONDO ROUNDHOUSE KICK is executed most often in three slightly different
ways. The first roundhouse uses the ball of the
foot as the weapon—the same weapon as a front
snap kick. This roundhouse is effective most
often to target the stomach area in close quar-
ters. You draw the toes back and, as you kick,
you twist the hips, but you don't produce the
same torque of the hips with this roundhouse as
you'd generate with other roundhouse kicks.
This kick is performed fast. Using this roundhouse lets you get in on someone who is well
guarded.

A straight-leg roundhouse uses the shin as the
weapon, not the instep. It is a powerful kick used
most often in full-contact fighting. To execute
this kick with the rear leg, bring that leg up without chambering. Using a lot of hip torque with
this kick can help you generate great power. The
straight-leg roundhouse is used in competitions
where leg kicks are permitted. The target for
these powerful kicks most often is the belly of
the hamstrings (the back of the legs). A low kick
like this is difficult to see, and eliminating the
chamber removes a lot of the movement that
telegraphs the roundhouse.

***To perform a rear-leg instep
roundhouse kick*** *with the left
leg, begin in a fighting stance.*

As you execute the kick, *the leg extends toward the target and the hips
twist to the right. After the kick, bring
your leg back into chamber and place it
on the ground. Chambering lets you
place the leg on the floor in a balanced
position.*

Lift the rear leg, bringing the knee to about a 45-degree angle *pointing
up and across the front of your body. Point the foot and toes downward, readying the instep weapon. The kicking leg is now chambered.*

44

The instep, or point-fighting, roundhouse, is the Taekwondo student's most familiar roundhouse kick. The weapon is a large bone at the top of the ankle group, called the talus. You can't get inside an attacker's guard with the instep roundhouse as you can with the ball-of-the-foot roundhouse. But an instep roundhouse can be effective against an attacker's knee, thigh, abdominal area, and head.

Basic Roundhouse Kick

To perform a rear-leg instep roundhouse kick with the right leg, begin in a fighting stance. Lift the rear leg, bringing the knee to about a 45-degree angle pointing up and across the front of the body. Point the foot and toes downward, readying the instep weapon. The kicking leg is now chambered. As you execute the kick, the leg extends toward the target and the hips twist to the left.

A straight-leg roundhouse uses the shin as the weapon, not the instep. From junbi, *begin by squaring the body to the target. At full speed, this step is performed very quickly and is hardly ever seen as such.*

Bring the rear leg up without chambering. Using a lot of hip torque with this kick can help you generate great power. The straight-leg roundhouse is used in competitions in which leg kicks are permitted. The target for these powerful kicks most often is the belly of the hamstrings (the back of the legs). Eliminating the chamber with this kick takes away a lot of the movement that telegraphs the roundhouse, and a low kick like this is difficult to see.

The roundhouse using the ball of the foot as the weapon is executed the same as the instep roundhouse. Draw the toes back and, as you kick, twist the hips. This kick is performed fast. Using this roundhouse lets you get in on someone who's well guarded.

Extending the leg and twisting the hips at the same time is important. After the kick, bring the leg back into chamber. Chambering lets you place the leg on the floor in a balanced position, or you can kick again, also from a balanced position. Keep your guard up while you kick—hold the fists near your face and keep your elbows close to your ribs.

Chambering the roundhouse is important for producing maximum power and maintaining your balance. If you arched your arm up from your side and struck a target with a straight arm, the strike would be only a weak push. Chambering—in this case cocking the arm at the shoulder and elbow—increases speed, and speed is an important part of power. If you don't chamber a roundhouse kick, the kick can still work for you, as it does in a straight-leg roundhouse, but the kick won't have the same power as a chambered kick.

Kicking Routines, Exercises

Working with a heavy bag and a kicking shield helps you increase your power. The focus pad is the smaller target, so it can be useful for improving your focus on a small targeted area. A focus pad is also beneficial for developing your speed and double-kick training. These training aids can also help you develop your sense of distancing—how far away you are and how close you need to be to the target to kick effectively.

Try these drills and exercises with roundhouse and other kicks. Practice these kicks as both front-leg and rear-leg kicks.

Heavy bag. Training with a heavy bag helps you develop timing. The bag moves as you kick, and when it moves back into range after one kick, as an attacker or an opponent would move, strike it again.

Two-person reaction drill. This drill helps you lessen reaction time and increase kicking speed. You and a partner face each other. As you throw a roundhouse kick, your partner blocks and kicks. As your partner kicks, you block and throw a kick immediately. This exercise is performed very quickly. It helps you maintain proper kicking form, and it helps you remember to keep your arms up and your elbows in as you kick.

Speed drill. Your instructor holds a kicking shield. You and a partner line up on either side of the shield. As soon as your partner kicks the shield, you kick. Immediately after you kick, your partner kicks. This drill and the two-person reaction drill are very demanding, but they help you kick faster and increasingly more accurately while maintaining proper form.

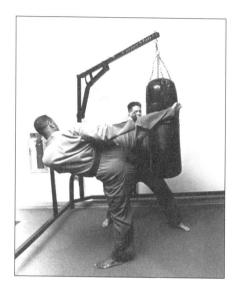

Training with a heavy bag helps you develop timing and power. The bag moves as you kick, and when it moves back into range after one kick—as an attacker or an opponent would move—you strike it again. A partner can occasionally steady the bag.

A two-person reaction drill is performed fast! It helps you lessen reaction time and increase kicking speed. You and a partner face each other. As you throw a roundhouse kick, your partner blocks and kicks. As your partner kicks, you block and throw a kick immediately. This exercise helps you maintain proper kicking form, and it helps you remember to keep your arms up and your elbows in as you kick.

A roundhouse kick speed drill is done fast! Your instructor holds a kicking shield. You and a partner line up on either side of the shield. As soon as your partner kicks the shield, you kick. Immediately after you kick, your partner kicks. This drill and the two-person reaction drill are very demanding, but they help you kick faster and increasingly more accurately while maintaining proper form.

Power drill. A partner or your instructor holds a kicking shield. In this drill, you move around repeatedly kicking the shield, making each kick as powerful as you can. This drill helps you learn the angles from which your roundhouse kicks are most effective. The drill is also beneficial when you need one strong technique either to score a point or disable an attacker.

Skipping drill. In this drill, you chamber the kicking leg and kick repeatedly, bringing the leg back into chamber but without dropping it. You proceed to "hop" the length of the training area. This drill helps you increase your balance and control while you are kicking. The drill is also useful when you face opponents who often retreat backward. As the opponents retreat, you follow, firing off kicks.

Strength & technique drill. You and your partner face each other, holding on to each other's shoulders and arms. One at a time you slowly go through the steps of performing a roundhouse kick. Then fire off a dozen or so quick kicks while still holding on to your partner for support. This drill is difficult and sometimes painful, but it is excellent for developing your strength, flexibility, and accuracy of technique.

Tension kicking. Support yourself on a bar or the back of a chair, and very slowly execute roundhouse kicks, dwelling several seconds at each step. Hold each step precisely and remember to perform each step very slowly. Like the strength and technique drill, this exercise helps you increase strength and flexibility, and sharpen technique.

In a power drill, your partner or your instructor holds a kicking shield. You move around kicking the shield, making each kick as powerful as you can. This drill helps you learn the angles from which your roundhouse kicks are most effective. This drill is also beneficial when you need one strong technique either to score a point or disable an attacker.

In a strength & technique drill, you and your partner face each other, holding on to each other's shoulders and arms. One at a time you slowly go through the steps of performing a roundhouse kick. Then fire off a dozen or so quick kicks while still holding on to your partner for support. This drill is difficult and sometimes painful, but it's excellent for developing strength, flexibility, and accurate technique.

Back-&-forth combination drills. You kick with a partner, moving through the length of your training area. Your partner defends, but moves in different directions and angles so that you also have to adjust your kicking position often. This drill helps you learn distancing as well as how to move and kick effectively from different angles.

Competition Strategies

In full-contact fighting and in point competition, if leg kicks are not allowed, it's best not to lead with a roundhouse.

In competition, the roundhouse kick's circular motion lets an opponent penetrate your defense if you execute a roundhouse as a lone lead attack. If you fire off a side kick, for example, straight ahead at your opponent, your body is positioned sideways and protected by your kicking leg. If a person comes in on you then, you can still catch the opponent with another kick.

Use a roundhouse in a double-kick combination, or as a second or third kick in another combination, or to set up another kick or combination. For example, execute a roundhouse, then a side kick, touching the ground with the kicking leg after the roundhouse. In this two-kick combination the roundhouse isn't meant to score—it's aimed at drawing the opponent closer with the slight opening that leading with the roundhouse provides. The side kick is meant to score.

The roundhouse works well as a second kick, especially in combination with a hook kick. For example, if you throw a hook kick to the head, you push the opponent in one direction and then return with a roundhouse from the other direction. This combination can surprise an opponent.

Front-leg roundhouse kicks are also good lead techniques in other combinations. For instance, you could perform some quick front-leg roundhouses followed by a reverse punch or a backfist. In this case, you draw the opponent's hands toward the abdomen so that you can score high with the hand techniques. Then you can score low again as the opponent raises his hands.

In this example, you execute the front-leg roundhouse, as a jab, repeatedly and quickly, so the opponent can't move in on you. Chambering the first roundhouse to strike harder requires you to execute it more slowly, and in that moment you're vulnerable to attack.

As you throw the front-leg roundhouse repeatedly, you sense the distance you need to strike your opponent and to evade his techniques.

Two kinds of double roundhouse kicks can be effective because they're quick and most competitors can perform them easily. In one double roundhouse combination, you execute the first roundhouse and, without lowering your foot to the floor, re-chamber and kick again. In the other double roundhouse, you execute the kick and, as soon as your foot touches the floor, you fire off the second roundhouse. This combination is kick, touch, kick, touch.

The first roundhouse kick in both double roundhouse combinations is a decoy. The second kick is your scoring technique, and it's much more powerful and precisely aimed than the first.

Both double roundhouse kicks are intended to move the opponent's guard away from the actual target. Double roundhouses can become triples and more, to draw the opponent's guard either upward or downward and to create an opening either high or low.

Self-Defense Application

The instep and ball-of-the-foot roundhouse kicks are the primary self-defense roundhouse weapons. These kicks let you target the lower legs most effectively—the outer or inner part of the knees, hamstrings, and inner thighs.

Rear-leg roundhouse kicks, either instep or ball of the foot, can also be very effective and can disable an attacker. These kicks can be even more effective when you are wearing shoes or sneakers.

9. Hook Kick

THE HOOK KICK can be effective in self-defense and in competition, but developing the kick's speed and power is the key to its effectiveness.

The hook kick's weapon is either the heel or the sole of the foot. To execute a rear-leg hook kick with the right leg, in a fighting stance, turn the body square and raise the rear leg as if you were chambering a front snap kick. Then turn your body as if were executing a side kick. Throw the kick as if it were a side kick, but just before you extend the kick fully, hook the sole of your foot or your heel into the target. After

Wearing down an opponent's guard *is one practical application of the hook kick in competition. Repeated hard hook kicks to the arms and shoulders will take their toll, and eventually the opponent will drop his guard.*

you've hooked the kick, bring it back into chamber and return to a fighting stance. Remember to keep your guard up as you kick, and don't let the arms flail.

When you execute a hook kick, the hips twist as they do when you throw a side kick or a roundhouse kick. When you throw the hook kick, you also torque the hip at the point of execution, pivoting on your support leg. This kick's driving force comes from turning the hips initially in the opposite direction of the kick. As you perform this kick, turn the hips in the opposite direction to create a more powerful pulling-in motion. This hip rotation means that the knee doesn't have to produce all the kick's power.

One main ingredient in this kick is pulling the kick back toward you just before you extend the kick fully. Don't perform the beginning side kick portion of this kick and extend the leg completely and then hook the kick, because this creates a weaker kick. You'd only be pushing the hook part of the kick, and it wouldn't have the power, speed, and snap that this kick needs.

As a whip snaps at the end of its motion, it is the snap at the end of this kick that determines its power.

Developing Power

Flexibility is the key to execute a hook kick properly if you target the head or another high target. Lack of flexibility forces you to "push" the kick, and it will lack the speed needed to generate power. If you're not flexible, learn the hook kick by focusing on low targets and work to develop the kick's form and proper hooking motion. The kick's speed and snap come only when you can perform the kick correctly, within your flexibility range.

Performing high hook kicks can stress the knees. Reducing the likelihood of injuring your knees requires strengthening the muscles and ligaments that support the quadriceps, the muscles that support the knees. Tension kicking, weight training, and flexibility training build the quadriceps.

Tension kicking is described more fully in Chapter 8. The technique works well with hook kicks.

The hamstrings help with the hooking part of this kick. Working with a partner is a good way to increase your hamstrings strength. First, hold on to a chair back, bar, or other support. Extend your foot nearly completely, as if you were executing a hook kick. Your partner supports your leg. Slowly and repeatedly perform the hooking motion of the kick while your partner provides resistance on your leg. Work in timed repetitions, first with light and then moderate resistance.

Shields, Focus Pads

Kicking shields and focus pads can also help you develop your hook kick. Kicking shields are useful in practicing kicks to the body, but the person holding the shield should let it "give" a little so you don't stress the knees.

Don't execute powerful hook kicks on a heavy bag. Like the kicking shield, this target needs to "give" so that the knees aren't stressed. Practice high hook kicks in the air to hone your technique. To develop focus and power, work with the kicking shield and focus pad.

Increasing your skill at hitting a moving target with a hook kick is best accomplished with shuffling drills. In a shuffle drill, your partner holds focus pads, one in each hand, and moves around, holding the targets in different places and at different angles and heights. You follow your partner, kicking the pads with combinations of front-leg, rear-leg, and spinning hook kicks.

To execute a rear-leg hook kick *with the left leg, start in a fighting stance.*

Turn the body square *and raise the rear leg as if you were chambering a front snap kick.*

Then turn your body *as if were executing a side kick.*

Street Strategies

The heel is the hook kick's weapon when you target the body or the legs. Targets include the knee, groin, inner thigh, and solar plexus. To strike the head, hit the target with the bottom part of the heel and sole of the foot as an attacker moves away from the kick. The kick extends more when you use the sole of the foot as the weapon.

You can strike an attacker's hamstrings with a powerful hook kick, and a low kick like this is difficult to block and see coming. A hard kick here can cause the hamstrings to spasm. You might also knock the attacker completely off his feet or disable his leg. If not, the kick can cause the attacker to face you, creating other openings for more devastating combinations.

A low, spinning hook kick, in which you use the heel as the weapon, can also be an effective sweep. Aim at the foot between the heel and the bottom of the calf. The spinning motion makes this kick effective by creating speed and power.

If an attacker isn't squared off to you, you can also attack his groin with a fast, strong hook kick.

Competition

Setting up another kick is a practical way to use a hook kick. In this case, the hook kick isn't powerful. You use it to bring the opponent toward the kick so that he is in range for the stronger next kick—this is exactly how you develop your scoring technique. For instance, you could throw a hook kick to the back of the opponent's body or back of the head to force him to turn toward you. Then you could execute a roundhouse kick immediately to the face or the body.

Bringing down or knocking away your opponent's guard is another tactic for which the hook kick can be used to great advantage. Direct a hook kick to the opponent's lead arm, as if you were knocking the arm away, or grabbing it and knocking it down. Then follow immediately with a front snap kick or a side kick to the open area of the opponent's torso.

Wearing down an opponent's guard is another practical application. Repeated hard hook kicks to the arms and shoulders will take their toll, and eventually the opponent will drop his guard.

Throw the kick as if it were a side kick, *just wide of the target.*

Just before you extend the kick fully, *hook the sole of your foot or your heel into the target. After you've hooked the kick, bring it back into chamber and return to a fighting stance. Remember to keep your guard up as you kick.*

Scoring with your first attack is possible with a quick front-leg hook kick, if you're flexible and quick. This technique works best if you see that your opponent lowers his guard, leaving his head open to attack.

With the front leg, the right leg in this case, throw a quick hook kick to the head. Practice this technique for speed, accuracy, and power with a partner holding focus pads.

A spinning hook is the technique used as the final element when you want to end a combination with a hook kick. An opponent can't easily see a hook kick to the back of the head. The opponent sees the kick appear to go wide, but then suddenly your hook kick connects to the head for a score.

Scoring with your first attack is possible with a quick front-leg hook kick, if you're flexible and quick. Practice this technique with a partner holding focus pads.

A hook kick is actually not for beginners. To perform it effectively you have to be able to execute a front snap kick and side kick correctly. Learning the hook kick too soon may turn your hook kick into a hooking side kick, which robs the kick of its power. Practicing hook kicks too early may cause you to hook all your kicks.

10. Crescent Kick

THE CRESCENT KICK is a versatile weapon both for competition and self-defense. In fact, when you consider that this kick has inside–outside and outside–inside versions, and that it can be executed with and without chambering the leg, it's actually several kicks grouped as one.

In addition, throwing the crescent kick doesn't require the tremendous amount of flexibility that some other kicks require. Of course, the more flexibility you have, the better. Still, the hamstrings and lower back muscles are the primary muscles used in executing a crescent kick. Other kicks require a great amount of hip and inner thigh flexibility. In most cases, a powerful crescent kick does the job when you might otherwise execute a wheel kick or a spinning hook kick.

The crescent kick is also unique. Most Taekwondo kicks evolved from the front snap kick and the side kick, Taekwondo's two basic kicks. But the crescent kick didn't come from either of those techniques. It evolved as a kick used primarily in competition, even though it has both competition and self-defense uses.

A crescent kick is most often used to knock down or brush away an opponent's guard or to bring the opponent's attention to the kick to set up another technique.

The attacker (left) executes a front-leg outside–inside crescent kick to knock down the opponent's guard.

The attacker reacts immediately by throwing a front-leg side kick to the open area of the opponent's head.

Outside–Inside

The crescent kick's outside–inside version starts with keeping the kicking leg slightly bent at the knee, and arcing it across the plane of the body from the outside of the body to the inside area, twisting the hips inward. The outside–inside version requires a lot of hip movement to execute powerfully. The weapon with the outside–inside crescent kick is the bottom of the foot.

The purpose of the outside–inside crescent kick is to knock down a person's guard or knock a weapon out of an attacker's hand. If you're close enough to your opponent and you have the flexibility, this kick can also be used to attack his head.

The outside–inside movement of this kick is also useful in setting up any kind of spinning kick. For instance, you could perform a combination of an outside–inside crescent kick to knock the opponent's guard away, or simply to draw attention to the kick, and then follow immediately with a spinning back kick to the open area of the opponent's torso.

The outside–inside crescent kick can also be performed by chambering the leg. When you chamber this kick, the weapon is the bottom part of the foot, and the motion of the kick is inward toward you and downward. You're using the kick as if you were grabbing downward with the foot, knocking the guard down. This technique is almost a hooking motion. In some cases, if you catch your opponent's hand at just the right angle, you can pull the opponent off balance with this grab-like technique.

Square your body to the target and raise the kicking leg, keeping it slightly bent at the knee.

Arc the leg across the plane of the body from the outside of your body to the inside area, twisting your hips inward.

The outside–inside crescent kick *with the rear (right) leg begins in a fighting stance.*

Keep the leg only slightly bent *as you place your leg down. The outside–inside crescent kick requires a lot of hip movement to execute powerfully. This hip motion would place you slightly turned as your foot touches the floor. The weapon with the outside–inside crescent kick is the bottom of the foot.*

Inside–Outside

Most people find the inside–outside version of the crescent kick more powerful than the outside–inside kick. That's because it doesn't require the same amount of hip motion as the outside–inside kick, and you can generate a lot more whipping motion and power with the leg. Some people can execute the inside–outside version quicker than they can throw the outside–inside kick, so the effect can be greater because of the speed this kick can generate. This is especially true when you execute this kick with the front leg.

The kick is executed practically the same as the outside–inside crescent kick. From a fighting stance, keep the leg slightly bent at the knee, and bring the leg up from the inside in a circular motion across the plane of the body toward the outside portion of the body. The weapon with the inside–outside crescent kick is the blade of the foot near the heel.

Like the outside–inside version, the inside–outside crescent kick can also be performed by chambering the leg. Of course, both kicks can be performed readily with either the front leg or the rear leg.

Competition

The usefulness of the crescent kick comes from its two versions, inside–outside and outside–inside. It is most often used to knock down or brush away an opponent's guard or to bring the opponent's attention to the kick to set up another technique.

For instance, as you spar, you and your opponent both have the right leg forward. You execute an outside–inside crescent kick with the front (right) foot, striking the opponent's right hand (the forward hand), knocking the right hand away from the body. Your momentum lets you spin quickly counterclockwise and throw a spinning back kick with your left foot to the open area of the opponent's midsection.

Keep your leg slightly bent at the knee, and bring the leg up from the inside.

Arc the leg in a circular motion toward the outside portion of your body. The weapon with the inside–outside crescent kick is the blade of the foot near the heel. Keep your leg slightly bent as you place it on the floor.

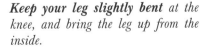

The inside–outside crescent kick with the rear (right) is executed practically the same as the outside–inside kick. Start in a fighting stance.

Combinations that include crescent kicks are also effective. For example, setting up as you did in the previous example, you could execute the outside–inside crescent kick with your right (front) leg but, instead of turning into the spinning back kick, re-chamber the right leg without letting it touch the ground and launch a side kick or a front snap kick to the open area of the opponent's midsection.

After executing the crescent kick, you could also touch your leg to the ground and with the same leg come back immediately with an inside–outside crescent kick to the opponent's head.

If you throw a series of crescent kicks to the opponent's guard and you notice that he drops his guard, you could also combine crescent kicks with hand techniques and other kicks to target his head.

At a more advanced level, you may perform three crescent kicks in a quick combination out-side–inside crescent to the guard, inside–outside crescent to the head, and outside–inside again to the head.

Self-Defense

One advantage of crescent kicks is their circular motion. In both competition and some self-defense situations, crescent kicks are a little more difficult to see coming than other direct kicks.

Furthermore, if an attacker threatens you with a knife, you might consider launching a direct kick designed to stop the attacker quickly, instead of attempting a combination. For this reason, you might consider a front snap kick or a side kick, both of which are direct and powerful. However, it's easier for an attacker to reach your leg with the knife if you throw these techniques right away.

Double crescent kick combinations can be very effective. Two competitors face off.

The attacker throws a front-leg inside–outside crescent kick to the opponent's head.

The crescent kick comes down only to touch the floor.

The attacker returns immediately with another crescent kick, this time an outside–inside kick again to the opponent's head.

A different defense uses a crescent kick that targets the back of the attacker's hand. In this case, you might execute an outside–inside crescent kick, so that you attack the hand holding the knife. Attacking from the outside reduces the chances of the attacker turning the hand toward your leg–it's easier to turn the knife inward than outward. For this reason, you would not choose an inside–outside crescent kick in such a situation as this.

Thus, defending with an outside–inside crescent kick might let you knock the knife out of the attacker's hand, or it might let you set up a decisive disarming or disabling technique.

Drills

Focus pad drills help you develop speed and power. You most often use crescent kicks to attack the hands and arms, so focus pads are best because they "give" as hands and arms do. For this reason, don't practice crescent kicks on a heavy bag.

In one stationary drill, your partner holds the focus pad as you kick, alternating one foot with the other. You'd throw all outside–inside crescent kicks, and then all inside–outside crescent kicks. You could also practice front-leg crescent kicks in a stationary drill. Throw five or 10 front-leg crescent kicks with the same leg. Once you're comfortable with the basic technique, increase the speed and power of your kicks.

Practice drills stationary before making them moving drills. In moving drills, follow your partner as he moves around. If your flexibility allows, in addition to moving around, your partner can change the height of the focus pad here and there.

In another drill, practice crescent kick combinations. With either the front leg or the rear leg, throw an outside–inside crescent kick and, when

Focus pad drills *help you develop speed and power. You most often use crescent kicks to attack the hands and arms, so focus pads are best because they "give" as hands and arms do. For this reason, don't practice crescent kicks on a heavy bag.*

the foot touches the ground, with the same leg come back immediately with an inside–outside crescent kick. Your partner should adjust the placement of the focus pad according to the combination you're trying.

Make up your own stationary and moving drill combinations with crescent kicks.

Stretching and Strengthening

Because you extend the leg straight out to throw a crescent kick, the hamstrings and the lower back muscles are the primary muscles used in executing crescent kicks. Remember that crescent kicks don't require as much flexibility to execute as do other kicks, so if you lack hip flexibility, you might want to use a spinning crescent kick instead of a wheel kick or a spinning hook kick.

11. Ax Kick

THE AX KICK is one of Taekwondo's most difficult kicks to control, so seasoned competitors don't use it often. Chopping down forcefully makes this difficult kick hard to hold back, and in competition if you try to hold the kick back once you've committed to performing it, you become vulnerable to counterattack. Nevertheless, the ax kick is a valuable weapon when you compete with a fighter who holds back–someone who lies in waiting more than becoming the aggressor.

The ax kick gets its name from the chopping motion of the leg. The weapon is most often the heel, but using the sole of the foot lets you reach a retreating opponent. The ax kick's most common targets are the top of the knee, point of the hip, chest, collarbone or shoulder, face, and top of the head.

Power & Speed

Executing this kick requires more speed and power than other kicks because you need to raise your leg quickly and pull it down forcefully. You can hone the chopping motion's accuracy, power, and speed by practicing with a partner holding a focus pad. Working the ax kick's power and speed is important be-

cause without power you can't chop down on the target forcefully, and without speed you're most vulnerable to counterattack.

Basic Execution

The ax kick might appear to be an easy kick to perform, but it's not. Most students begin practicing the ax kick early because straight high kicks, or front-rising kicks, performed during class kicking drills, easily become ax kicks when you begin chopping the leg down forcefully on the target.

Even though straight high kicks aren't taught as ax kicks during kicking drills, they help students stretch and strengthen the hamstrings.

Hone the ax kick's chopping motion for accuracy, power, and speed by practicing with a partner holding a focus pad. Working the kick's power and speed is important because without power you can't chop down on the target forcefully, and without speed you're most vulnerable to counterattack.

They also help you learn to keep the body upright and balanced as you execute the kicks.

To perform an ax kick with the rear leg– the right leg in this example–start in a fighting stance with the right leg back. As you bring the leg up, rotate the hips square and then toward the left. The knee is slightly bent, but not chambered. Raise the leg in a slight arc, almost as if you were performing an inside–outside crescent kick. As you begin chopping down onto the target, twist the

To perform an ax kick with the rear leg–the right leg in this example–start in a fighting stance with your right leg back.

As you bring the leg up, rotate the hips square and then toward the left. The knee is slightly bent, but not chambered. Raise the leg in a slight arc, almost as if you were performing an inside–outside crescent kick.

As you begin chopping down on the target, twist the hips back to the right. The kick can also be performed by arcing the leg from the outside in.*

hips back to the right. The kick can also be performed by arcing the leg from the outside in.

You can chamber an ax kick as you'd chamber a crescent kick. Doing so adds a whipping motion to the kick, but adding another motion telegraphs the kick more and reduces its chopping motion. Even though chambering this kick is possible, it's best not to.

Competition

Because the ax kick requires a lot of motion, telegraphing it can be a problem. You reduce the chances of telegraphing this kick if you perform it with the front leg in a fighting stance. Even though you are attempting an ax kick with the front leg, you could turn this kick into a front snap kick to the chin.

One way to set up an ax kick is to direct the opponent's attention either to the left or right and perform an ax kick to the other side. For example, you could begin by jabbing with the left hand or throwing left-foot front kicks.

Then perform an ax kick with the right leg, arcing from the inside to the outside, striking the opponent's left shoulder or the left side of his chest.

You could also try a combination of mid-level front snap kicks to make the opponent lower his guard. When he does, try an ax kick. The opponent may think you're coming with another front kick, but your ax kick looms high and chops down on the opponent's unguarded head or chest.

Set up an ax kick in competition with mid-level jabs and kicks.

As the defender lowers his guard, execute an ax kick to his upper body.

Self-Defense

If you're not highly skilled with an ax kick, don't try it in self-defense. Still, if the ax kick becomes one of your favorite weapons because you perform it well, an attacker might not expect it. In addition, a beginner who is very flexible can learn to use an ax kick well because it's basically a stretching kick. Most people who are less flexible in the inner thighs have more flexibility in the hamstrings. They can often perform an ax kick better than they can execute side kicks and roundhouse kicks. With a front snap kick, the ax kick is actually one of the easier self-defense techniques.

High targets are the same as those used in competition, but in self-defense targeting lower parts of the body can also be effective. For instance, effective self-defense targets for the ax kick include the area of the quadriceps and the area just above the knees.

In self-defense, targeting lower parts of the body with an ax kick can be effective. Self-defense targets for the ax kick include the area of the quadriceps and the area just above the knees.

Jam the Ax Kick

You can defend against an ax kick by jamming. This means that when your opponent begins to execute the kick, you close the gap, diminishing the ax kick's effectiveness. In this case you might counter with hand techniques. Remember that an ax works best with defensive competitors, who are likely to retreat instead of closing the gap and jamming.

Avoiding the kick is another defense. Sidestep the kick or move out of range, and when the opponent brings the leg down—remember that controlling this kick is difficult—counter immediately.

12. Spinning Kicks

A SPINNING BACK KICK, spinning hook kick, and spinning wheel kick can be effective in self-defense and in competition. But even though you may be able to perform these kicks in class, making them effective to win points against a shrewd, prepared opponent, or against an attacker, is another story. You need flawless technique and accurate evaluation of your opponent's skill, and you need your own flexible, varied strategy on when to use these more advanced weapons.

Basic Execution

To perform the spinning back kick or the spinning hook kick, begin in a fighting stance. As you begin to turn the torso and head to see the target, bring the knee of the kicking leg up into chamber. At the point where you twist, begin shooting out the spinning back kick and the spinning hook kick.

Re-chamber the kick.

Shoot out the spinning back kick *or the spinning hook kick. The foot position for the spinning hook kick and spinning back kick are the same. However, when you perform the spinning hook kick, as you shoot out the kick you hook it inward, as if you were grabbing the target with your foot.*

To perform *the spinning back kick or the spinning hook kick with the rear (left) leg, begin in a fighting stance.*

Turn the torso and head *counterclockwise to see the target.*

Bring the knee of the kicking leg *up into chamber as you turn.*

Return *with the left leg back in a fighting stance.*

The torque you generate from quickly turning gives these kicks more power than stationary kicks. The foot position for the spinning hook kick and spinning back kick is the same. However, when you perform the spinning hook kick, as you shoot out the kick you hook it inward, as if you were actually grabbing the target with your foot.

The weapon in the spinning back kick is the blade of the foot near the heel. The spinning hook kick's weapon is the heel or the sole of the foot.

The spinning wheel kick begins the same as the spinning back kick and spinning hook kick, except that as you turn your head and torso, instead of chambering the kicking leg, you bring the leg up in more of a circular motion with the knee only slightly bent. The same torque generated by quickly spinning gives the wheel kick much power.

Spinning kicks are more advanced techniques, because if you don't kick quickly and in a balanced position you open yourself greatly to counterattack. For this reason, practice spinning kicks with a front-leg side kick that immediately follows the spinning kick. In this way, if you miss the target, your opponent's counterattacking is more difficult.

Competition

Don't begin a combination with a spinning technique, and don't perform one in competition by itself. You create much forward momentum, especially with the spinning back kick and the spinning wheel kick. Starting your attack this way means you have to crouch a little, and this movement readily telegraphs your intent. In addition, executing spinning techniques requires your full commitment to the attack. If the opponent unbalances you as you execute a spinning kick, you may not land in a position that lets you counter.

Strike the target in a circular motion. Drive through the target without stopping the motion of the foot.

The spinning wheel kick with the left leg begins in a fighting stance, the same as the spinning back kick and spinning hook kick.

Turn the head and torso counterclockwise to see the target.

Instead of chambering the kicking leg, bring the leg up in more of a circular motion with the knee only slightly bent. The torque generated by quickly spinning gives the wheel kick much power.

Return with the left leg in a fighting stance.

The best way to hide your preparation to execute a spinning technique is to keep moving–shuffling the feet, and ducking the head and moving it from side to side. This movement doesn't let an opponent read your intention easily. You mask your intention to perform a spinning technique even more when you include spinning kicks with other techniques.

Even though beginning a combination with a spinning kick isn't practical, in certain defensive situations starting with a spinning technique can be effective. You may be successful in this case if an opponent lunges, or blitzes, often, and it may work for you if your opponent charges often with hand techniques. You execute the kick when your opponent begins to execute a punch. You time the spinning technique so that you land it as the opponent's momentum brings him into the kick as he executes the punch or blitz.

A spinning wheel kick might work for you when your opponent moves away as he fights. As you perform the spinning wheel kick, your leg extends a little farther and you can often catch the opponent as he backs away from you.

Set up the spinning wheel kick by throwing one or two other kicks, like front-leg round-houses or side kicks. As he begins moving away from you, launch the spinning wheel kick.

Similarly, a spinning hook kick and a spinning back kick are useful when an opponent comes toward you, or when he comes after you in an offensive combination. When the opponent commits to a scoring technique, you can execute the spinning hook kick or the spinning back kick, letting his forward momentum work for you.

To determine if you can use spinning techniques effectively, you have to weigh an opponent's ability. As you move around, consider how fast an opponent moves, and notice whether he uses more hand techniques than kicking techniques. Fighters who favor punches often generate much forward momentum to score, so setting them up with spinning back kicks and hook kicks may be easier than setting up other fighters with different styles.

Execute the kick *when your opponent begins to throw a punch. You spin counterclockwise here to land a left-leg spinning back kick.*

Time the spinning back kick *so that you land it as the opponent's momentum brings him into the kick as he executes the punch.*

Even though beginning a combination with a spinning kick *isn't practical, in certain defensive situations starting with a spinning technique can be effective. You may be successful in this case if an opponent lunges, or blitzes, often, and it may work for you if your opponent charges often with hand techniques.*

In this example you would spin clockwise to perform a right-leg spinning wheel kick. Your leg extends a little farther, and you can often catch the opponent as he backs away from you.

A spinning wheel kick may work when your opponent moves away as he fights. Set up the spinning wheel kick by throwing one or two other kicks, like front-leg roundhouses or side kicks. As the opponent begins moving away from you, launch the spinning wheel kick.

Spinning Kick or Jump-Spinning Kick?

A jump-spinning technique may work in many situations in which you would use a spinning technique. Jump-spinning kicks, more advanced techniques than spinning kicks, let you cover much more ground than spinning techniques.

Jump-spinning kicks are also stronger than spinning kicks, and generate more forward momentum. Jump-spinning kicks increase your power and range beyond that of spinning kicks and stationary techniques.

When you consider using spinning techniques, remember also that the spinning back kick and the spinning hook kick are protective. Your arms remain close to the body as you crouch, spin, and chamber the legs. If your opponent is fast and sees the kick coming, his forward momentum causes you to run into his hip and your kick will be jammed. However, your guard still protects your head and body, so the opponent isn't likely to score on you in this circumstance.

Self-Defense

Many competitive uses of spinning kicks can work in self-defense. Because you must be very proficient with spinning kicks to use them successfully, practice spinning kicks with an immediate follow-up technique, like a front-leg side kick or a jab. This follow-up makes countering a missed spinning technique more difficult. Furthermore, in self-defense an attacker may see you turn to begin a spinning technique and think you're retreating. When an attacker sees you retreat, he'll likely come after you—which can make your spinning technique even more effective.

Your skill, conditioning, and assessment of your opponent or attacker have to be their highest if you want to score in point sparring with spinning techniques or defend yourself successfully. Still, put everything together well and spinning techniques can be your winning edge.

13. Punching, Hand Techniques

THE THREE MOST BASIC PARTS of Taekwondo punching and other hand techniques are learning first to make a fist properly, executing techniques correctly, and then learning how to use the body–the shoulders and hips–with the techniques. For everyday classes, competition, and self-defense, no special conditioning of the hands or fingers is required.

Knowing how to execute the techniques and when to use them is important because Taekwondo incorporates many hand techniques. Consider the most basic and most prac-

tical hand techniques, how to perform them correctly, and how and when to use them.

- **Reverse punch.** A traditional reverse punch is executed with the back hand (not the lead hand). This powerful punch incorporates turning the shoulders and hips, and twisting the fist at the point of execution to contribute a measure of additional power and focus. A reverse punch is effective when you strike the nose, mouth, throat, and abdominal area.

The reverse punch's weapon is the knuckles of the index and middle fingers (arrows).

A traditional reverse punch is executed with the back hand (not the lead hand) from a fighting stance.

This powerful punch incorporates turning the shoulders and hips, as well as twisting the fist at the point of execution to add a measure of additional power and focus.

Making a Fist

With your hand open, close the space between the fingers as they are outstretched and then slowly curl them down as if you were squeezing an imaginary air pocket held in your palm. Place the thumb across the index and middle fingers, squeezing the fingers for support.

The weapon of the fist for the reverse punch, vertical punch, back-fist, and jab is the knuckles of the index and middle fingers. These two knuckles naturally become the weapon because they are more supported by the arm bones than are either the ring finger or the pinkie.

Such traditional horse-stance punching, that is so pervasive throughout Taekwondo training, is a particularly valuable technique. It allows you to develop proper timing and retraction, and also teaches you how to twist the fist. As well, it lets you concentrate on keeping your wrist straight.

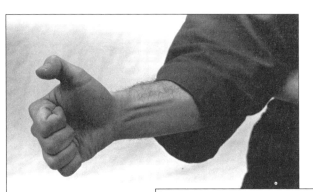

With the hand open, *close the space between your fingers as they are outstretched and then slowly curl them down as if you were squeezing an imaginary air pocket held in your palm.*

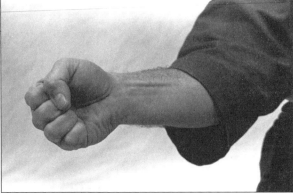

Place the thumb across *the index and middle fingers, squeezing the fingers for support. The weapon of the fist for the reverse punch, vertical punch, back-fist, and jab is the knuckles of the index and middle fingers. These two knuckles naturally become the weapon because they are more supported by the arm bones than are either the ring finger or the pinkie.*

In class, competition, and self-defense situations, make sure that you always keep your fists closed tightly and your thumbs pressed firmly out of the way.

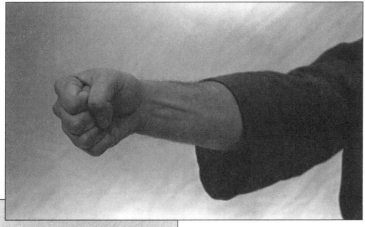

- **Straight vertical punch.** This punch is also executed with the back hand. It's performed the same way as a reverse punch except that the fist remains upright—you don't twist the fist at the point of contact. This punch is effective when striking the side of the body or the ribs.

The straight vertical punch is also executed with the back hand. It's performed the same way as a reverse punch except that the fist remains upright. Don't twist the fist at the point of contact.

The straight vertical punch's weapon is the same as that of the reverse punch—the knuckles of the index and middle fingers.

- **Jab.** The jab isn't a particularly powerful punch. The lead hand snaps out and back with the same kind of twisting motion as a reverse punch. The jab is a setup technique. The better boxers are those with excellent jabs—they keep the jabbing fist in the opponent's face, and that often confuses him and lets you set up other combinations. The corkscrew motion of executing the technique can tear the opponent's skin.

To execute the jab, snap the lead hand out and back with the same kind of twisting motion as is used in a reverse punch. The weapon is the knuckles of the index and middle fingers.

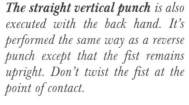

The back-fist weapon is the knuckles of the index and middle fingers.

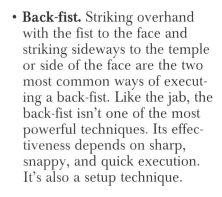

To execute a back-fist, strike overhand with the fist to the face or sideways to the temple or side of the face.

• **Back-fist.** Striking overhand with the fist to the face and striking sideways to the temple or side of the face are the two most common ways of executing a back-fist. Like the jab, the back-fist isn't one of the most powerful techniques. Its effectiveness depends on sharp, snappy, and quick execution. It's also a setup technique.

• **Hook punch.** A hook can be executed with either hand in a fighting stance, but from the back hand a hook is more powerful because you can put more of your body into the punch. You twist the body and shoulders to perform a hook punch with either hand, but you direct the hips and shoulders inward, not straight ahead as you would with a reverse punch or vertical punch.

A hook punch can be executed with either hand in a fighting stance, but from the back hand a hook is more powerful because you can put more of the body into the punch. Twist the body and shoulders to perform a hook punch with either hand, but direct the hips and shoulders inward, not straight ahead as you would with a reverse punch or a vertical punch. The weapon is the first two knuckles of the index and middle fingers.

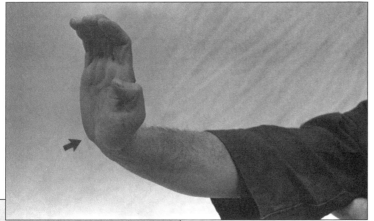

• **Palm-heel strike.** This strike targets areas in the center of the body—primarily the nose, chin, and solar plexus. A palm-heel strike is executed as a reverse punch and straight vertical punch, except that the weapon is the bottom part of the palm. Keep the thumb in tightly and hold the fingers together, slightly bent. When you target the face, rake the fingers downward after the strike.

The palm-heel strike's weapon is the bottom part of the hand (arrow). Keep the thumb in tightly and hold the fingers together, slightly bent. When you target the face, rake the fingers downward after the strike.

• **Uppercut.** This punch is powerful. You target the chin, but you can also strike the solar plexus and floating rib effectively. The weapon is the first two knuckles.

*A **palm-heel strike** is executed like a reverse punch and straight vertical punch.*

*The **uppercut** is a powerful punch. Target the chin, the solar plexus, and the floating rib. The weapon is the knuckles of the index and middle fingers. For maximum power, turn the shoulder and hips into this punch .*

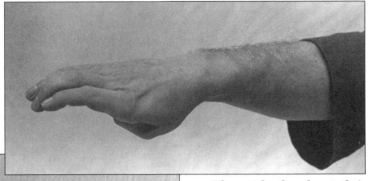

The ridge-hand strike's weapon is the bone that extends from the index finger knuckle to the wrist.

The ridge-hand strike is performed downward or straight across, in both cases with a slight circular motion. The strike from the outside inward is the most powerful. The strike is executed much as you'd perform a hook punch, with the hips and shoulders directed inward with the strike. The ridge-hand's power comes from the hips and shoulders.

• **Ridge-hand strike.** This technique is performed downward or straight across, both with a slight circular motion. The weapon is the bone that extends from the index finger knuckle to the wrist. The strike from the outside inward is the most powerful. The strike is executed much as you'd perform a hook punch, with the hips and shoulders directed inward with the strike. The ridge-hand's power comes from the hips and shoulders.

• **Hammer-fist.** The hammer-fist can be a powerful technique. The weapon is the bottom of a tightly clenched fist from the fingers to the wrist. With the hammer-fist you might target the collarbone, face, and, depending on the circumstances, joints like the knees, elbows, and wrists.

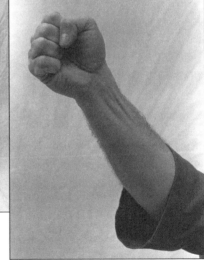

The hammer-fist can be a powerful technique. With the hammer-fist you might strike the collarbone, face, and, depending on the circumstances, joints like the knees, elbows, and wrists.

The weapon is the bottom of a tightly clenched fist from the fingers to the wrist.

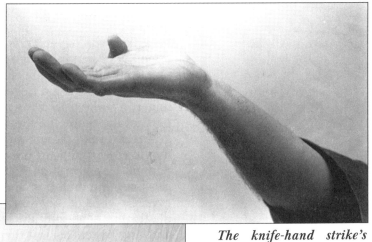

• **Knife-hand *(Sudo)* strike.**
Knife-hand strikes can be performed most often with the palm upward, which directs the strike inward across the plane of the opponent's body, or with the palm down, which directs the strike outward. *Sudo* strikes frequently target the neck or throat. The weapon is most often the bottom part of the hand from the lowest part of the pinkie to the wrist. However, with proper conditioning, more powerful *sudo* strikes are those that use the bone from the bottom of the pinkie to the wrist.

The knife-hand strike's weapon is most often the bottom part of the hand from the lowest part of the pinkie to the wrist. However, with proper conditioning, more powerful sudo strikes are those that use the bone from the bottom of the pinkie to the wrist.

Knife-hand strikes can be performed most often with the palm upward, which directs the strike inward across the plane of the body.

Knife-hand strikes can also be performed with the palm down, which directs the strike outward. Sudo strikes frequently target the neck or throat.

Generally speaking, for head strikes, techniques using the palm-heel, ridge-hand, hammer-fist, and knife-hand may work better than punches. Punching techniques work best on the body.

The hammer-fist is a valuable self-defense technique for attacking the shoulder or collarbone. No matter how big or how strong an attacker may be, the collarbone protrudes and breaking it isn't difficult if you strike the middle of the bone. Even striking the shoulder with your hammer-fist can be effective, and chances are, you won't hurt your hand.

The hammer-fist is a valuable self-defense technique for attacking the shoulder or collarbone. No matter how big or how strong an attacker might be, the collarbone protrudes and breaking it isn't difficult if you strike the middle of the bone. Even striking the shoulder with your hammer-fist can be effective, and chances are, you won't hurt your hand.

Punching techniques work best when you target the body. The attacker (left) grabs the defender. He responds with a straight vertical punch to the attacker's ribs.

14. Blocks

Blocks are the first Taekwondo techniques taught, along with stances. This suggests the defensive character of Taekwondo. There are many blocks taught in Taekwondo training. Here are the most practical ones for competition and self-defense.

- **Down block.** This technique is often the first block taught. It's often taught first from a front stance. If a student learns the block first, the block is performed in the *junbi* ready position.

Practice the arm motion first. Blocking with the left hand, bring the left fist to the right ear. Cross the centerline of the body with your right arm, the right fist facing downward. Imagine somebody grabbing your right wrist, preparing to kick you. Block downward as if you were stripping the attacker's grip from your right wrist and blocking a kick.

A down block is taught traditionally to block a front snap kick, but it can also be used to block any attack to the lower part of the body.

Down block. *Practice the arm motion first, starting in* junbi.

Blocking with the left hand, *bring the left fist to the right ear. Cross the center line of the body with your right arm, the right fist facing downward.*

Imagine somebody grabbing your right wrist, *preparing to kick you. Block downward as if you were stripping the attacker's grip from your right wrist and blocking a kick.*

To perform an outside–inside left forearm block, make fists and cock the left arm slightly, bringing the fist near the left shoulder. Move the right arm across the abdomen. Move the left forearm from left to right, and snap the right fist into chamber. The left arm finishes at shoulder height, the left fist aligned with the center part of the body. The left palm faces you. The retraction obtained with the right arm adds power and snap to this block. The weapon is the inside part of the forearm from the wrist, three or four inches up the arm.

To perform an outside–inside left forearm block, from junbi *make fists and cock the left arm slightly, bringing the fist near the left shoulder. Move the right arm across the abdomen.*

Move the left forearm from left to right, *and snap the right fist into chamber. The left arm finishes at shoulder height with the left fist aligned with the center part of the body. The left palm faces you. The retraction obtained with the right arm adds power and snap to this block.*

• **Knife-hand blocks.** These blocks are similar to the down block and the inside–outside forearm block, except that you're blocking with the knife part of your open hand—the outside part of the palm from the base of the pinkie to the wrist. Form a knife-hand with the non-blocking hand, and position it palm up at the navel. In the traditional practice this hand guards the lower portion of the body as you perform the low, middle, and high knife-hand blocks.

When performing the middle and high knife-hand blocks, keep the elbows in, facing downward to protect the ribs. A common error in performing these blocks is that some students hold the blocking arm nearly parallel to the ground. The block might be effective, but positioning the arm this way opens the body and ribs to attack.

In the high knife-hand block, the blocking hand finishes so that the thumb is parallel to the nose. When performing the middle and high knife-hand blocks, keep the elbow of the blocking arm in, facing downward to protect the ribs.

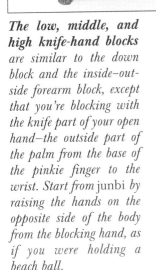

The low, middle, and high knife-hand blocks are similar to the down block and the inside–outside forearm block, except that you're blocking with the knife part of your open hand—the outside part of the palm from the base of the pinkie finger to the wrist. Start from junbi by raising the hands on the opposite side of the body from the blocking hand, as if you were holding a beach ball.

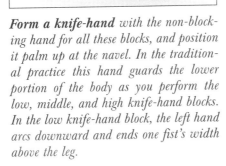

Form a knife-hand with the non-blocking hand for all these blocks, and position it palm up at the navel. In the traditional practice this hand guards the lower portion of the body as you perform the low, middle, and high knife-hand blocks. In the low knife-hand block, the left hand arcs downward and ends one fist's width above the leg.

In the middle knife-hand block, the blocking hand finishes so that the thumb is parallel to the chin.

• **Leg blocks, checking.** To perform a leg block, simply raise a leg into chamber. This technique is effective against groin attacks and other low kicks. It allows you to block the attack without lowering your guard, which would create an opening to your upper body and head.

Checking is blocking with your feet. It is a jamming technique with which you cut short an attack. You prevent an attacker or competitor from extending a kick toward you.

For instance, as an attacker lifts a leg to kick, you perform a low side kick, striking the attacker's kicking leg just below the knee. Checking this way jams the attack and often unbalances the attacker.

To perform a leg block, simply raise a leg into chamber (left). This technique is effective against groin attacks and other low kicks. It lets you block the attack without lowering your guard, which would create an opening to your upper body and head.

Checking is blocking with your feet. It's a jamming technique with which you cut short an attack. You prevent an attacker or competitor from extending a kick toward you. In this example, the attacker (right) lifts a leg to kick, but the defender performs a low side kick, striking the attacker's kicking leg just below the knee. Checking this way jams the attack and often unbalances the attacker.

Drills

The purpose of drills in Taekwondo training, and in all martial-arts training, is to develop your blocks into perfectly timed reactions. This is what allows you to bring the benefits of class training into competition and into self-defense. You may have the cleanest, sharpest blocking technique, but if you don't continuously hone that technique through drills and practice, you won't react quickly enough in competition or in a self-defense situation.

Blocks are learned best alone with stationary drills and with a partner in moving drills. Blocks are often practiced with stance drills. At first, to learn each blocking technique, execute the block in a variety of stances, beginning from a *junbi* ready position. Performing stationary drills in front of a mirror lets you check positions and stances as you perform blocks.

Don't practice moving drills with a partner to check a block's power. Moving drills are best for developing timing and control. In moving drills you block, moving backward or forward, as your partner kicks or punches. You progress from one kind of attack parried by one kind of block, to combinations of attacks and blocks.

Moving drills are best for developing timing and control. In moving drills you block, moving backward or forward, as your partner kicks or punches. You progress from one kind of attack parried by one kind of block, to combinations of attacks and blocks. From junbi *with two partners facing each other, the attacker (right) steps forward and punches in a front stance while the defender steps backward in a front stance and blocks.*

Next, the attacker (right) steps forward again *and punches with the other hand, while the defender steps backward again and blocks with the other hand.*

Timing

Timing is vitally important in blocking. For instance, a common bad habit among some students is that when they see a kicking technique coming–any technique–they automatically lower the hands in a down block. This reaction is a bad habit; if the technique isn't directed to the lower portion of the body, lowering the arms creates a large opening to the upper body and head.

In competition and in self-defense, the confidence that comes with learning correct timing means that when someone simply lifts a leg or flinches, you won't automatically lower your guard. Blocking drills help you learn to wait until an opponent commits to an attack. Through blocking drills, you combine a honed sense of distancing, knowing simply when to get out of the way, blocking with the legs, and sharp timing of your blocks.

Through drills you also learn to transfer the power of traditional techniques into the more fluid, practical applications in competition and in self-defense.

Attacking the Attack

Think of blocking techniques as strikes–striking the attack. You attack the attack with your defensive block. In this way you increase the chances of causing enough pain with your block to end the attack. You might not even have to strike back.

15. Elbow Strikes

Elbow techniques are not permitted in open competition. But in close-quarters self-defense, elbow strikes can be most effective. In fact, in some tight situations executing powerful, fast punches and kicks may not be practical. In these circumstances, using elbow strikes effectively can stop an attacker, create opportunities to launch other disabling techniques, or give you the chance to retreat.

This may be the reason why elbow strikes abound in traditional Taekwondo forms, and in the forms of other styles. Over hundreds of years martial artists who created and modified what have become Taekwondo techniques realized the significance of honing many different elbow techniques.

The elbow itself is a weapon, but the area about three inches from the tip of the elbow down the forearm is also an elbow strike, even though it's not specifically the elbow. The end of the ulna, one of the two forearm bones, is actually the elbow. The weapon three or four inches above the elbow is a wider part of the same bone.

The elbow itself is a weapon, *but the area about three inches from the tip of the elbow down the forearm is also an elbow strike, even though it's not specifically the elbow. The end of the ulna, one of the two forearm bones, is actually the elbow. The weapon three or four inches above the elbow is a wider part of the same bone.*

Point the palm toward the body when performing a forward elbow strike, and keep the fist tight. Point the palm upward to strike behind you with the elbow. Point the palm behind you to strike downward or upward with the elbow.

Conditioning

Condition the elbows to reduce the risk of injury as you learn and practice elbow techniques. This kind of conditioning is different from conditioning the side of your hand or the knuckles for breaking. Elbow conditioning is best accomplished by using focus pads, the heavy bag, and light board-breaking (one or two boards). This kind of conditioning shows you how to strike with the elbow in a variety of ways, and specifically which parts of the elbows are the weapons. You also learn how to avoid accidentally striking your "funny bone" as well as how to avoid other improper, ineffective elbow strikes. Conditioning exercises such as light board-breaking and working with a heavy bag also allow you to evaluate how strong your elbow strikes are.

Instead of punching the heavy bag, strike it with your elbows and upper forearms. Striking the bag this way requires you to be closer to it than you would be if you were punching or kicking. The heavy bag also helps you develop proper distancing because all elbow strikes are performed close to the target.

Do you have trouble developing the hip-turning that's important to performing a strong reverse punch? Use forearm and elbow strikes instead of punches, and rotating the shoulders and hips properly may thereby come easier for you. When you practice elbow strikes on a heavy bag, you develop the hip and shoulder rotation that's vital to executing powerful punches and elbow techniques.

As you work with a heavy bag, turn and spin so that you strike the bag from different angles. Use elbow techniques behind you, in front of you, and to your sides. Remember to move around the bag, too.

You hone your speed and power with elbow strikes when you work with focus pads. Have a partner position pads high and low, and at different angles, so that you have to strike upward, downward, straight ahead, to your sides, and behind you. You and your partner should work as many possibilities with elbow strikes as you can. You increase your speed and decrease your reaction time with these kinds of focus pad drills.

Strategies

Elbow strikes aren't usually considered blocks. However, when someone directs a side kick, front kick, or roundhouse kick under your arm or toward your ribs, striking downward with the elbow turns the block into a strike. You may know how painful getting caught with an elbow in the foot can be.

The body's bony parts are the most likely targets for elbow strikes. Elbow strikes to the temples, solar plexus, ribs, and jaw can be more damaging than punches.

You hone your speed and power with elbow strikes when you work with focus pads. Have a partner position pads high and low, and at different angles, so that you have to strike upward, downward, straight ahead, to your sides, and behind you. You and your partner should work as many possibilities with elbow strikes as you can. You increase your speed and decrease your reaction time with these kinds of focus pad drills.

Instead of punching the heavy bag, strike it with your elbows and upper forearms. Striking the bag this way requires you to be closer to it than you would be if you were punching or kicking. The heavy bag also helps you develop proper distancing, because all elbow strikes are performed close to the target.

Then, with your right elbow, *strike upward to the attacker's chin.*

Then strike downward *with the back part of the elbow onto the attacker's face.*

An attacker (right) attempts a right-hand reverse punch. Block with the left arm and step closer to the attacker.

Suppose an attacker attempted a right-hand reverse punch. You'd block with the left arm and step closer to the attacker. Then with your right elbow you'd strike upward to the attacker's chin, and then downward with the back part of the elbow onto the attacker's face. Similarly, suppose an attacker grabbed

your right shoulder with his left hand. You'd step closer and with your left elbow strike the attacker's jaw.

In both instances, closing the gap prevents the attacker from mustering the full force of a punch or kick. You'd also follow the elbow techniques here with finishing combinations, or you would retreat.

An attacker (right) grabs your right shoulder with his left hand.

Step closer, *preventing the attacker from mustering the full force of a punch or kick, and trap the arm— unbalancing the attacker.*

With your left elbow, *strike the attacker's jaw.*

Consider the defense against the bear hug *from behind. Reacting before the attacker could throw you to the ground or lift you off your feet is important to defend successfully against this classic attack. Drop straight down into a low horse stance and lift your elbows, breaking the attacker's grip, or at least diminishing its effectiveness.*

Then execute an elbow strike *to the attacker's ribs or solar plexus. The target in this case would be whatever is in range of your elbow technique.*

Consider also the bear hug from behind. Reacting before the attacker could throw you to the ground or lift you off your feet is important to defending yourself successfully against this classic attack. You'd drop straight down into a low horse stance and lift your elbows, breaking the attacker's grip, or at least diminishing its effectiveness. Then you would execute an elbow strike to the attacker's ribs or solar plexus. The target in this case would be whatever is in range of your elbow technique.

As you practice elbow strikes with a heavy bag and with a partner holding focus pads, you discover that the possibilities for elbow strikes in close are practically limitless. The martial artists who formulated today's Taekwondo and other styles also knew this idea. That's why Taekwondo forms and the forms of other styles incorporate a wealth of elbow techniques.

Heed this wisdom. In close, when kicking and punching might lose their power and effectiveness, remember your elbow strikes.

16. Deadly Groin Strikes

IN SOME TRADITIONAL TAEKWONDO FORMS, and in the forms of other styles, low blocks, low knife-hand blocks, and low pressing blocks can be interpreted as defenses against groin strikes. Other forms that Taekwondo stylists practice, including *Chong Moo, Koryo, Bassai,* and *Kanku,* contain *sudo* groin strikes and groin-tearing techniques. The powerful beginning movement of *Bassai*–lowering the two hands directly in front of the body–can be interpreted to be a pressing block, defending against a groin strike. *Bassai* also includes chambering a leg to protect the groin from a kick, as do the forms *Pyung Idan* and *Pyung Samdan.*

This history of practicing groin strikes and blocks in forms suggests that over the centuries no one had to tell martial artists that the groin is a vital self-defense target, and that attackers would attempt groin strikes.

Groin strikes aren't allowed in point fighting or in Olympic-style competition. In real self-defense, however, the groin appears to be an obvious target, but it isn't such an easy spot to hit squarely. The groin is actually a small target, and an attacker usually moves constantly. Unless an attacker stands still in an open stance, connecting with a groin shot that abruptly ends

a confrontation isn't a certainty. Furthermore, the adrenaline that flows during a fight lets some people continue even after taking an apparently well-placed groin kick or punch. This is especially true when an attacker is under the influence of drugs that suppress pain.

These basic Taekwondo techniques *can be used to defend against groin attacks. The techniques appear in traditional Taekwondo forms and in the forms of other styles. They are (left to right) a low knife-hand block, chambering the leg, and a low pressing block.*

For these reasons, groin strikes can be practical, and they should certainly be part of your Taekwondo self-defense repertoire. But to be effective, groin strikes require precision, skill, and lots of practice.

Setting Up the Attacker

To set up a groin strike, if the attacker chooses not to wrestle you to the ground, you must make him square off, or create your own opening that exposes his groin. Hard roundhouse kicks to the back of the leg can cause an attacker to start twisting toward the pain to protect the leg. This squares the attacker's body to you and opens the groin area to your attack.

When an attacker squares off to you, one effective technique is a hard, thrusting front snap kick. Even if you don't connect, the power of the kick might still cause a lot of pain in the lower abdomen. The lower abdominal area just above the groin is a difficult area to condition, so a hard kick there could help you set up an attacker for another strike, or it might give you the opportunity to retreat.

When an attacker squares off to deliver a punch or a kick, a straight lifting kick with the instep may also be effective. The snap kick and the straight lifting kick can work with either the front leg or the rear leg, but you need speed and accuracy to execute these kicks effectively during that brief moment when the attacker squares off to you.

If the attacker is positioned in a side fighting stance, somewhat protecting the groin, a very hard ball-of-the-foot roundhouse kick to the groin may also work.

Another way to create an open groin shot is to target the inner thigh of one leg with an instep roundhouse kick. During the instant the attacker squares off to you after you've delivered the roundhouse, re-chamber the kick and follow immediately with a mule kick (heel) to the groin.

An experienced defender could also move under an attacker who tries a high kick, throwing a side kick to the attacker's groin.

As you practice groin attacks and combinations that lead to groin strikes, don't assume that the defense finishes with the groin shot. Train to include other techniques after you've delivered a groin strike. For example, if you move under a high kick and execute a side kick to the attacker's groin, continue with another groin strike, target the attacker's knee, or execute a takedown.

As the attacker (left) squares his body *to the defender, the defender follows immediately with a mule (heel) kick to the exposed groin.*

The defender (right) repeatedly targets *the inside of the attacker's leg. This creates an opening for a groin kick by making the attacker square off.*

The defender follows the last roundhouse kick immediately with a hook kick to the attacker's leg, making the attacker square off further.

The defender follows the hook kick right away with a side kick to the attacker's exposed groin.

The defender (right) creates another opening for a groin strike by making the attacker square off. First, the defender strikes the back of the attacker's leg with a series of roundhouse kicks. The attacker begins to square off by moving the leg backward in reaction to the painful roundhouse kicks.

Using the Hands

Hands aren't usually the weapon used in groin strikes. However, if an attacker throws a high kick and you have enough experience and speed, you can block, go under the kick, and strike the groin with a hand technique.

Similarly, if an attacker attempts a side kick, evade the kick by moving sideways. Then, as you trap the kicking leg, strike the attacker's exposed groin with a palm-heel or a ridge-hand. A similar defense appears in the traditional Taekwondo form *Pyung Odan*. With your left hand you block a left-leg roundhouse kick to the right side of your face while executing a right-hand fingertip knife-hand strike to the attacker's groin.

You could apply a similar response to a punch. As you block a right-hand punch with your left hand, with your right hand strike the attacker's groin with a ridge-hand or palm-heel.

You could also block the kick or punch, and then with your hands grab the attacker's shoulder and back of the neck. Then draw the attacker down and into a knee strike to the groin.

The defender (left) steps out of the way of the attacker's side kick. The defender traps the leg and strikes the attacker's groin with a ridge-hand.

Protecting the Groin

Someone who goes for the groin is usually the defender, not the attacker. Attackers usually go for the head or the body, or the attacker tries to take you to the ground. Nevertheless, protecting the groin in any confrontation is still vital.

The key to protecting the groin is not to square off to an attacker. When you are confronted by an attacker who chooses not to grapple right away, remain in a side stance, fighting stance, or even a more traditional Taekwondo back stance so that the attacker cannot easily strike your groin.

You should keep your guard up to protect both sides of the face. That means keeping the fists tight and up. To protect both sides of the body, keep the elbows in close to the ribs. An attacker may likely go for your body or your knees. With training and experience, you maneuver so that you don't give an attacker a clean knee strike, or open leg or hand shot, to your groin, and your hands guard the head and your upper body.

In point-fighting, you might fight with one hand protecting the face and one hand down, protecting the groin. In competition, an opponent isn't coming at you full-force trying to hurt you. Some control is required, so you and your opponent take a little power off each technique. However, in street self-defense, if you hold one hand down near the groin, you protect it but give up protecting the rest of your body.

For this reason, it's best to keep your guard up and chamber the legs to protect the groin against kicks, as in *Bassai, Pyung Idan,* and *Pyung Samdan.* In *Bassai,* the leg is raised into chamber.

Straight Talk About Groin Cups

A groin cup is the most vital male training item for protecting the groin. There are basically two kinds of groin protectors. Flat, or conventional, cups are designed primarily for baseball, football, and other sports. They are designed to protect you against a straight-on blow to the front of the body. However, Taekwondo practitioners and other martial artists require the additional protection against strikes rising from below the groin.

For this reason, a tuck, or contoured, cup is designed to give martial artists more protection. A tuck cup simply curves slightly more under the body than a flat cup. Groin protectors that are made specifically for boxers, which afford hip and kidney protection, are not tuck-under cups, and they are for the most part too cumbersome for Taekwondo use.

A cup should fit comfortably and snugly. The supporter, in which the cup is placed, is the key to a proper fit. Supporters are sized according to waist measurement. A properly fitted supporter should hold the cup firmly in place. When your cup starts to move around in the supporter, it's time to buy a new supporter. Supporters loosen through wear and washings. A loose-fitting cup can injure you.

A groin cup is designed to provide vital protection and, in most cases, it does that. Wearing a groin cup in training is like wearing a seatbelt in an automobile. Wearing one is decidedly prudent, and it's the first step toward lowering your risk of injury, but it is certainly no guarantee against injury. You must also understand a cup's limitations, exercise appropriate control in training, and fit a cup and supporter correctly.

The next movement, a hammer-fist strike next to the chambered leg, can be interpreted as a strike meant to break the attacking leg near the ankle. In *Pyung Samdan,* the leg is chambered, protecting the groin, but it's followed with a side kick.

In street self-defense, you open yourself to a groin strike by throwing high kicks. Unless you are very quick with a high kick, and you strike the target squarely and decisively, you are vulnerable.

In responding to a bear-hug attack, the defender (right) repeatedly strikes at the attacker's groin with hammer-fists.

Painful Truth

Why is a groin shot so incapacitating?

"The pelvic area of both men and women holds many nerves—what's referred to as 'complex innervation.' When you take a groin shot, these nerves are stimulated and you experience a very wide range of symptoms," says Mark Mascari, a Harrisburg, Pennsylvania-based D.O. and Taekwondo student. "Nerve impulses starting in the groin not only send pain sensation to the brain—they also stimulate the intestinal tract to spasm. This noxious stimulation of the pelvic area's complex innervation can even slow the heart rate to the point at which the victim may become faint."

Treatment

"Most blunt trauma to the groin area can be treated with rest, ice or cold packs and in males, scrotal elevation," says Dr. Mascari. "In females, vaginal laceration can occur, and quick treatment is required to prevent infection and chronic dysfunction. Anti-inflammatories like acetaminophen, aspirin or ibuprofen can also be helpful.

"Any pain in the groin area lasting more than an hour following a strike warrants a consultation with a physician, even with no other symptoms."

Dr. Mascari suggests the following signs that indicate a medical emergency resulting from a groin strike and that prompt an immediate visit to an emergency room:

- seeing blood on urination or the presence of blood at the opening of the urethra

- immediate swelling of the scrotum in males, or a laceration of the labia or vagina in women

- scrotal pain, or its red or bluish discoloration

- a red, hot, hard mass at or near the groin that's painful to the touch

Furthermore, Mascari says, reflex innervation may also induce profuse sweating, and may cause the blood vessels to dilate, dropping the blood pressure and thus causing faintness.

"Both males and females have the same innervation," Mascari says, "but males may feel more discomfort because of the pendulous nature of their genitalia and the greater shearing forces that can be placed on them. These greater shearing forces cause more traction and stimulation of the nerve endings."

Always remember–protect your groin, be sure that you do not square off to an opponent in class, in competition, or on the street, and be certain that you chamber a leg against a groin kick rather than give up guarding your upper body by lowering your hands. Consider the necessity inherent in including groin strikes and blocks in traditional Taekwondo forms. If you find yourself in a confrontation, remember that groin strikes work, but you have to strike accurately, powerfully, and quickly.

17. Leg Take-downs

Martial arts tournaments are often held in gymnasiums with hardwood floors. Years ago, competitors used support-leg, rear-leg, and double-leg take-downs so effectively that injuries on these gymnasium floors were common. Today, for this reason, rear-leg and double-leg sweeps are not allowed in point competition.

Competitors today are allowed to use front-leg sweeps in point competition, but to properly score a point you must follow the sweep with a point-scoring technique. Sweeping simply to take someone's legs out from under him is not permitted.

Sweeps are not allowed in Olympic-style Taekwondo competition, either. These tournaments focus on kicking, and competitors who know they might be open to a leg take-down are cautious about lifting a leg to kick.

Today's tournament rules, and the safeguards that are inherent in them, show how effective sweeps—leg take-downs—are for competition and for self-defense.

A soft, narrow blocking target works well when practicing sweeps because it "gives." A partner can hold the target firmly on the floor to simulate an attacker's leg. Spring-loaded targets work this way, too.

The target in most sweeps is the back of the leg between the heel and the bottom of the calf muscle.

Competition

Front-leg sweeps in open competition are most often roundhouse-like motions with either the front or the rear leg. A successful front-leg sweep causes the opponent to press his legs rigidly downward while lowering his guard. This position creates an opening for a point-scoring technique. A front-leg sweep in competition isn't meant specifically to break the opponent's balance, but in some cases the sweep does just that. Nevertheless, a competitor who executes a successful sweep has to follow immediately with another technique to score a point.

A scissor take-down is also allowed in point competition. To score a point, you must also follow the scissor take-down with another technique. Scoring techniques that follow a scissor take-down most often include a roundhouse kick, ax kick, or side kick, depending on whether you take the opponent down on his chest or on his back.

To perform a scissor take-down, use your stronger leg to take the opponent down, and that leg should be on top. The other leg is used more for tripping, even though both legs do perform a "scissors" motion.

Execute a scissors take-down first by starting in a fighting stance. Step forward with the front leg, and push off with the back leg, jumping into a "scissors" position. Position your strong leg at the front of the opponent's waist. Place the other leg above the knees at the hamstrings. In this position you take the opponent down on his back. If you were taking the opponent down on his chest, you'd place the top leg waist level on the opponent's back, with the lower leg on his quadriceps.

Executing a sweep as a lead technique against an opponent who's well guarded and prepared is difficult. For this reason, setting up a sweep with other techniques is the best strategy. Draw the opponent's (above right) attention away from the legs with mid-level punches or kicks.

Sweep the opponent's front leg with a rear-leg roundhouse kick. If the kick doesn't sweep the opponent off his feet, he may temporarily lose his balance, dropping his guard.

Score with a technique to the open part of the upper torso or head.

As you extend your legs, "scissor" the opponent and torque your hips in the direction you want him to fall. Keep your bottom leg rigid. If the bottom leg collapses, the technique will not work.

To learn a scissor take-down, use a building's support beam or post. Practice pushing off and jumping into position for the take-down. As you touch the beam or pole, land in a side fall.

Of course, you cannot practice the follow-through with a stationary object. But the important part of the technique is jumping into the correct position and falling properly. You have to get used to performing these otherwise awkward movements to add a scissor take-down to your arsenal. Whether you take an opponent down on his back or on his chest depends on your body position, the opponent's body position, and the specific setup techniques you use.

You can execute a roundhouse motion to take an opponent down on his chest. Use a hook-kick motion to effectively scissor an opponent down on his back.

Competition Strategy

If you find that you can consistently get close to an opponent, a scissors take-down or a front-leg sweep may work well. Size up the opponent by throwing front-leg side kicks and roundhouse kicks as you move around. The opponent may block the kicks, but if you touch him with each kick, keep firing off front-leg side kicks and roundhouses. As you do so, your opponent may think that you are just kicking as usual when you launch the scissor take-down.

With an experienced competitor, don't try this more than once. In this case, if you've used a scissor take-down or other sweep successfully, use the possibility of launching another sweep to set up other scoring combinations.

Executing a sweep as a lead technique against an opponent who's well guarded and prepared is difficult. For this reason, setting up a sweep with other techniques is the best strategy. For example, to perform a sweep to the opponent's front leg with your rear leg, use low and mid-level punches and kicks first. These let you drop low easily as you spin and sweep.

In point sparring, a legal front-leg sweep might cause an opponent to fall.

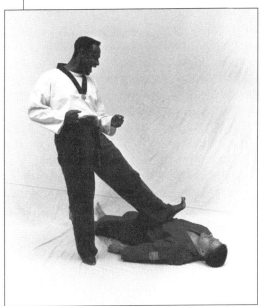

To score a point, you must follow the sweep with a point-getting technique. In this case, the attacker (left) finishes with an ax kick.

In this self-defense scenario, the defender (left) squares off with an attacker.

The attacker tries a spinning back-fist, which the defender blocks.

The defender traps the arm immediately and breaks the elbow.

You might also want to draw the opponent's attention high and then sweep low. Throw mid-level or high spinning kicks. Then as you spin again, your opponent might expect and prepare to block a mid-level or high attack as you execute a low spinning sweep.

Sweeps also work with competitors who rock back and forth on their feet in one place. Time the sweep when the opponent shifts most of his body weight to the front leg. In this case, completely unbalancing the opponent and sending him to the floor with a front-leg sweep is possible.

More Sweeps

A soccer-style sweep is a very effective self-defense weapon. If you are behind an attacker for an instant, use a low roundhouse-like motion with the inner part of either foot, following through on the motion, as if you were kicking a soccer ball. Strike the back of one or both legs, between the heel and the calf. Pull the attacker down from the hair or shoulder at the same time as you sweep. Even if you strike only one foot, the combination of sweeping and pulling the attacker down is often enough to drive him to the ground.

A soccer-style kicking sweep sends the attacker to the ground.

Other take-downs use hook kick motions and roundhouse kick motions that sweep the opponent's feet inward. Remember that these techniques are leg take-downs. They are different from hip throws, trips, and other techniques that put an attacker on the ground.

If you find you can consistently get close to an opponent, a scissors take-down or front-leg sweep might work well. Execute a scissor take-down first by starting in a fighting stance. Step forward with the front leg, and push off with the back leg, jumping into a "scissors" position.

Position your strong leg at the front of the opponent's waist. Place the other leg above the knees at the hamstrings. In this position you take the opponent down on his back. As you extend your legs, "scissor" the opponent and torque your hips in the direction you want the opponent to fall. Keep the bottom leg rigid. If the bottom leg collapses, the technique won't work.

In competition you must perform a scoring technique immediately after a scissor take-down to win a point. In this case, the attacker (right, as seen in this reverse-angle photo to better show the technique) scores with an ax kick.

Sweeps and Self-Defense

An untrained attacker is often fully committed to a punch or a kick, and focuses solely on the target–your face or stomach, for instance. He doesn't consider balance and stance as you do. If you dropped low and swept, you might surprise this attacker, taking his feet right out from under him.

Defending Against Sweeps

Your opponent may attempt to sweep you, especially if you attempt the technique. One effective defense is to keep moving unpredictably in all directions–shuffling from side to side and in and out. Sweeping an elusive target is more difficult than sweeping a stationary or predictable opponent.

Even though this self-defense situation is idealized, take-downs are often unexpected. They can end an attack, or give you some time to follow up–especially if the attacker is injured in the fall. Sweeping effectively also gives you time to retreat.

Even if an attacker knows you know how to kick, he might expect a mid-level or high attack. The assailant might be unprepared if you spin low and sweep his legs.

A double-leg take-down can be effective if you observe an attacker with his feet close together. A quick, powerful double-leg take-down brings the attacker's feet upward and drives his head and shoulders to the ground. Remember also that an attacker who has not trained to learn how to fall will likely injure himself as a result of the fall.

Practicing

A soft, narrow blocking target works well when practicing sweeps because it "gives." A partner can hold the target firmly on the floor to simulate an attacker's leg. Spring-loaded targets work this way, too.

18. Sparring

SEVERAL KINDS OF COMPETITION attract Taekwondo stylists. These include point sparring, Olympic-style sparring and kick-boxing, also called full-contact fighting. Point sparring offers the beginner the best initial avenue into competition.

In point-sparring competition you must wear foot and hand pads. Headgear is often required below the black-belt level. Light contact to the body is allowed, but no contact to the head is permitted. After a judge thinks a point was scored, fighting is stopped. Below the black-belt level, the first competitor to score three points wins.

Competition usually includes a center judge, who controls the match, and four corner judges who call out points and infractions. At least three of the four corner judges must agree for a point to be awarded. The first competitor to score three points wins.

The attacker (left) *tries a blitzing back-fist to the opponent's head, which the defender blocks. The block creates an opening to the midsection.*

The attacker follows quickly with a reverse vertical punch to the ribs.

The attacker continues with an overhand left hook to the temple.

Competitors begin in a ready position.

The attacker (left) attempts a blitzing back-fist to the opponent's temple, which the opponent blocks.

As the opponent reacts to the back-fist, the attacker delivers a front-leg side kick to the open rib cage.

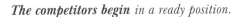

The competitors begin in a ready position.

Watch point-sparring competition winners closely, and time and time again you'll see that *basic* techniques—not more difficult spinning and jump-spinning techniques—are their main arsenals. Of course, these competitors can execute and score with remarkably technical and difficult combinations. And they certainly do that. But more often than not, by themselves a jab and reverse punch combination, a quick, strong side kick, and a jab-like front-leg side kick score points and create champions.

Your skill level determines the techniques you use in competition. If you're a beginner, first build a strong foundation with basic techniques. This lets you put more difficult techniques and combinations into your fighting arsenal as you advance. As you progress, remember that simple techniques aren't simplistic, and that "back to basics" is a saying that winning competitive experience repeatedly confirms.

Point-Sparring Strategy Basics

You could probably find someone on the street and teach him to execute one punch or one kick. In point sparring, throwing one kick, one punch, or one block is easy. When an opponent steps back into a fighting stance at the beginning of the match, that competitor is well guarded and

can probably block, or at least minimize the effect of, any single technique. So when you're kicking and punching, your goal is to perform combinations of techniques that create openings in the opponent's defense.

You accomplish this by throwing some high techniques, and then some low ones—going "high, low, high, low." In this way, when you draw the opponent's attention low, strike high for the point. When you draw his attention high, strike low for the point.

There is an infinite number of quick combinations you can execute to create openings. Some are complicated, but most are simple, with one or two setup techniques and then a point-getter.

Consider blitzing techniques first. For instance, you execute a quick back-fist followed immediately with a middle punch or front snap kick. You have to execute blitzing techniques quickly and commit to them totally. If the opponent doesn't block the first technique, even though the first technique isn't meant to be the point-getter, you still score. But the opponent's blocking the technique, or at least moving an arm up or down in the direction of the attack, creates the opening for the second, stronger point-getting technique.

From a ready position, *the attacker slides the back foot forward to close the gap between him and the opponent.*

The attacker *knocks the opponent's front guard down, which creates an opening to the jaw.*

The attacker lands a reverse punch *to the attacker's open face.*

Shuffle

Experienced competitors are not easily fooled by blitzing techniques. Blitzing attacks require you to charge forward–which telegraphs your intent to an experienced fighter. In this case, your opponent could sidestep your attack, counter with a kick to the body coming beneath your arm, or simply retreat.

For this reason, it can be to your advantage to learn how to throw combinations while you are shuffling. Flat-footed opponents are easier to hit squarely than are fighters who move constantly. In addition to making you a more difficult target to strike, shuffling keeps you balanced, ready to attack or defend.

From a ready position, *the attacker (left) shuffles forward and fires a back-fist to the opponent's head, which the opponent blocks.*

As the opponent blocks the diversionary back-fist, *the attacker twists around and attempts a rear-hand reverse punch to the opponent's solar plexus, which the opponent blocks.*

The attacker follows *immediately with a front snap kick to the open rib cage.*

There are many ways to shuffle. In one kind of shuffling, you repeatedly move the back leg forward to the front leg. You do this only momentarily and randomly, because if you're caught with your feet together, or if you develop a rhythm, an alert opponent might sweep you. Still, occasionally moving your back foot toward your front foot creates a distraction. Your opponent doesn't sense your purpose—it just appears as if you're simply moving around. The opponent can't readily see your actual intent: closing the gap between you and him so that you can launch an attack.

After you successfully close the gap, follow up immediately. One practical tactic is first to launch a diversionary back-fist. This technique isn't the point-getter. You throw this punch to make your opponent react—block or raise the arm—creating an opening to launch a more forceful point-scoring attack to the open target.

What if your opponent isn't fooled by the diversionary back-fist? Keep throwing techniques until you do create an opening.

You have to practice combinations that work for you. This means using techniques that you favor—techniques that fit your flexibility and skill level. The idea is to shuffle and put together combinations of punches and kicks. This is "mixing it up." Skilled competitors confuse opponents this way and create openings.

Try these drill combinations to get started:

- Two jabs, a reverse punch, and a side kick.
- A jab, reverse punch, and front kick, followed by a reverse punch and a jab.
- A front-leg side kick, jab, spinning back kick, and a jab and reverse punch.
- Crescent kick (knocking down the opponent's lead guarding hand), back-fist.
- Two crescent kicks, spinning back kick.
- Double roundhouse kicks (kick–touch–kick).

Practice these drills alone first—in front of a mirror and then on a heavy bag. When you're comfortable stringing three or four techniques together, work on executing longer combinations; but remember that basic techniques are more often than not point-getters.

You might want to throw a retreating side kick or back-fist at the end of your combinations. Execute these techniques at the end of combinations as you begin to move away from your opponent's reach. As the opponent counterattacks, these retreating techniques can sometimes score points by surprising an unprepared opponent. They can also foil his counterattack and create another opening for you.

From a ready stance, *the attacker (left) attempts a back-fist to the temple, which the defender blocks.*

The defender then tries a reverse punch *to the midsection. The attacker deflects the punch with a pressing block that holds the opponent's guard down, creating an opening to the head.*

The attacker follows *quickly with a front-leg hook kick to the head, which the opponent is unable to block.*

Setting

Timing is important, too. No matter what you do in combinations, you can't launch techniques without first setting. "Setting" is the instant you plant both feet squarely on the floor at the moment of your attack. You can punch and kick when you don't set, but those techniques will be weak and unbalanced.

Skilled competitors set very quickly, so the most experienced fighters shuffle to hide their setting. You can hardly see a seasoned competitor's setting, but it is there. Stationary competitors telegraph setting the most—often in the movements of the shoulders and hips.

Even though skilled fighters set very quickly, everyone is open to attack during setting. If you're quick and you can time your opponent's set, you can score first by executing combinations at the moment the opponent sets, just before he launches an attack; or you can at least prevent an opponent from getting off a technique against you.

Your style, skill, and body structure determine the kinds of combinations you perform. The key to success is to keep moving—shuffling—and working basic techniques into your fighting combinations. Set up more advanced moves first by using combinations of basic techniques. Either way, let your basic techniques help you score, no matter how far you progress in rank.

Olympic Taekwondo Competition

Consider Olympic-style Taekwondo competition when you reach at least the intermediate level. To succeed in Olympic-style Taekwondo you need to maintain control, form, and solid skills throughout a match, especially when you tire. Olympic-style fighting is more difficult than point-fighting. It requires more kicking skill and the ability to focus power.

In Olympic-style competition you don't wear the traditional safety equipment you wear in point sparring. You compete with bare hands and bare feet except for the insteps. You wear cloth shin, groin, forearm, and instep protectors under the uniform, and you must wear a white uniform with a traditional V-neck top. Headgear and a chest protector are also required. These items must be approved by the United States Taekwondo Union (USTU) or by the organization that represents your country in the World Taekwondo Federation (WTF). The USTU is the organization representing the United States in the WTF. You have to be affiliated with and approved by your state-representing president to compete in sanctioned tournaments.

Full contact to the body is allowed. You score points by striking certain designated areas of the torso. However, unless you execute a technique that causes the opponent to move, you're not awarded a point. To score a point, you must convince the judges that if the opponent weren't

Olympic-style Taekwondo tournaments incorporate standard rules and specific uniform requirements.

Courtesy of Bill Waite

Courtesy of Bill Waite

wearing protection, your technique would hurt him. The only hand techniques you can score with are traditional straight reverse punches that cause the opponent to be displaced.

After each technique that scores a point, the match continues—fighting isn't stopped, as it is in point sparring.

There are two outside judges and a referee who controls the match. The referee doesn't award points. Whoever earns the most points wins, unless there is a knockout. A tie or a score-less match goes to the referee, who decides which fighter was the more aggressive and more effective. An arbitrator sits and watches and can overrule the awarding of points.

Olympic-style competition is fought in rounds. The number and duration of the rounds depend on the level of the competition—local, state, or national. Competitions most often include two to three rounds of one to two min-utes. Point-sparring tournaments can be spon-sored by anyone.

Olympic-style competition has now achieved medal sport status in the year 2000 Olympics. The competition was a demonstration sport in the 1992 Olympics.

Taekwondo is mostly kicks, so Olympic-style fighting encourages the art of kicking. Only kicks to the body that displace the opponent are point-getters, so competitors use a lot of quick, strong kicks—rear-leg roundhouse kicks, spin-ning back kicks, and ax kicks. Setup kicks, like a front-leg side kick, and hand techniques are exe-cuted, but no hand techniques to the head are permitted, even though you're allowed to kick the head with contact to the helmet area.

Olympic-style Taekwondo is not like point sparring—if you kick someone in the head in point sparring, you're disqualified. Furthermore, you can't punch to the face in Olympic-style competition, so competitors don't often perform hand techniques.

The only similarity between point sparring and Olympic-style Taekwondo is in some of the setup techniques. Olympic-style Taekwondo requires more endurance because you don't stop fighting until the round ends. Point sparring stops with each point, and that provides a rest.

Olympic-style Taekwondo uses eight weight classes in male and female divisions to ensure the fairness of a match. There are more weight divisions in Olympic-style sparring than in point

Even judges must undergo training to participate in USTU-sponsored events.

Courtesy of Linda Spotts

Courtesy of Linda Spotts

sparring. Olympic-style fighting is based more on specific weight classes rather than experience. In point-fighting, there are male and female divisions, which are further divided by age, experience (rank), and weight.

In Olympic-style Taekwondo, competitors chamber techniques less than they would in point sparring, using instead more straight-leg kicks. Straight-leg kicks can be performed faster and more quickly than chambered kicks, and they can cause more damage. In point sparring, chambering kicks can draw an opponent's guard down for a point—competitors aren't kicking for power, so a chambered kick can shoot higher or lower. Point sparring is more like tag—tagging the open target. Olympic-style fighting is more power related. You want to kick hard to score a point.

In Olympic-style Taekwondo, the hands are often held out with the arms down. The powerful ax kick can work with fighters chest to chest, so competitors hold their arms out to prevent an opponent's using an ax kick. Because punching the face is against the rules, keeping the guard up is not always necessary.

Except for the development of kicking technique, Olympic-style Taekwondo is not self-defense related. However, one benefit of Olympic-

style Taekwondo is that competitors learn to follow through and see the effect that their kicks or punches have. However, learning the other part of fighting is important, because otherwise you can develop bad self-defense habits, including letting your arms hang. For street self-defense, of course, you want to develop the reaction of keeping your guard up.

Consider the benefits of Olympic-style Taekwondo training. You learn the more realistic training of following and hitting someone moving, as well as how to throw a technique to get a strong reaction. You learn to read an opponent and to understand the benefits and the consequences of commitment to a technique. You also learn what it is like to get hit.

Point sparring teaches many useful self-defense skills, including timing and distancing. But the tag-like nature of point-fighting teaches you to pull techniques. For this reason, work with kicking shields to develop the follow-through with your techniques. All-control and air-kick conditioning can leave you without the ability to know how to make contact.

Elements of both sports are useful. You might want to work both sports so that you develop an all-round competitive habit with effective self-defense skills.

Full-Contact Fighting

Full-contact fighting, or kick-boxing, is a combination of Olympic-style Taekwondo and point sparring. Full-contact fighting takes point sparring to the next level, where you're not focusing on pulling your techniques. For instance, when you execute a back-fist, jab, or reverse punch to the face, you're trying to do more than just make your opponent react—you're trying to hit the opponent. Full-contact fighting uses the regular boxing ring. The same safety equipment as point sparring is required, with boxing gloves. There are rounds and knockouts, and boxing scoring is used. A decision is rendered if there is no knockout or the fight isn't stopped.

More Information on Olympic-Style Competition

For more information on Olympic-style Taekwondo, contact the **U.S. Taekwondo Union (USTU)** at:
One Olympic Plaza,
Colorado Springs, CO 80909
phone: (719) 578-4632
fax: (719) 578-4642

19. Forms Practice

FORMS ARE ARRANGED sequences of the basic techniques in which you defend yourself against several imaginary attackers. Forms practice is a large part of Taekwondo training because it encompasses all aspects of the art. Forms practice begins at the earliest stages of Taekwondo training. However, you will reap the greatest benefits of practicing forms at advanced levels of training, after practicing progressively more difficult forms over a very long period.

Forms practice begins at the earliest stages of Taekwondo training. *However, you reap the greatest benefits of practicing forms at advanced levels of training, after practicing progressively more difficult forms over a very long period.*

Forms practice is vital for four reasons:

- **First,** practicing forms helps you develop technique. Each new form you learn includes basic techniques. Some techniques are new, and techniques that appeared in forms you've already learned are used in the new form in different combinations.

- **Second,** practicing forms increases your balance and helps you learn to move effectively. No one stands still in competition and in self-defense. In forms you move and turn in all directions. Forms practice gradually lets you turn rigid, traditional combinations of techniques into increasingly more balanced, fluid, powerful fighting movements.

- **Third,** as you develop the ability to focus, execute combinations, and move in a variety of directions you learn to understand the applications of each technique in a form. Forms are designed as self-defense tactics, so forms practice teaches you to react effectively when you're attacked. The more you understand each movement's and combination's applications, the easier it becomes to execute forms, and performing them becomes quicker, sharper, stronger, and more balanced.

- **Fourth,** forms practice lets you combine all your Taekwondo skills. Forms are designed to take you as close to real self-defense as possible without risking a lot of injury.

This sequence shows the first five movements from a starting position of the traditional Taekwondo form Pyung Chodan.

As you advance in Taekwondo, forms practice helps you develop an appropriate, skilled reaction to whatever happens. Beginning forms include foundation-building techniques and, as you progress, forms include increasingly more advanced techniques and complicated movements.

Forms in a Jar of Peanut Butter

A skilled Taekwondo practitioner performs forms fluidly, powerfully, and with a lot of "snap." There is more to achieving this level of skill than simply repetitive practice. One beneficial way to practice all your forms is to perform them in very slow, powerful, concentrated movements. That is, you perform each technique in the entire form as if you were submerged in a jar of peanut butter.

Tense every muscle. Control your breathing. Perform every movement in extra-slow motion, breaking down each technique into its component parts. Snap every kick, block, and punch at the end of each technique. (Continued in box on the opposite page.)

You condition the body to move in many different ways and in many different directions against imaginary attackers, so that when you are actually attacked, you react with one of the pieces of the forms you know. Any trained reaction is better than no reaction or an unskilled reaction.

Forms practice also prepares you for competition because it fosters a "can do," winning attitude.

Learn new forms in pieces—a quarter, a third, or a half at a time. First learn the form's rough movements. Then, as you continue to practice the form, dissect the form so that you understand each movement and combination.

Then practice the form occasionally with other students attacking, so that the form becomes more realistic.

This extra-slow practice builds your strength and flexibility. It is also exhausting. More important, it helps you develop the ability to focus your power to specific weapons at the end of each technique, where you want each technique to be most powerful.

If you're a beginner, no one expects you to understand how to direct your power to a weapon. But when you practice forms this way, you become accustomed to feeling the snap at the end of the technique and to directing your attention to each weapon.

Practicing forms this way also shows you the point to which you should direct your power. It helps you learn this advanced skill.

This sequence shows the same first five movements *from a starting position of* Pyung Chodan, *but with an attacker.*

As you continue to practice forms over a long period, your rigid performance will become faster, more balanced, more powerful, and more fluid–just like real combat. Apply these ideas to all the forms you know and to new forms that you are taught. This kind of training allows you to make your forms practice into real self-defense training, and remember that it applies to all forms at all skill levels.

First, learn a form's rough movements. *Then, as you continue to practice the form, dissect the form so that you understand each movement and combination. Then practice the form occasionally with other students attacking, so that the form becomes more realistic.*

20. Breaking & Developing Practical Skills

Will this technique work against an attacker?

Students often ask this question. But how can you test the effectiveness of Taekwondo techniques short of actually hurting someone in a realistic self-defense scenario?

Breaking boards is one way of testing the effectiveness of your techniques. The prima-

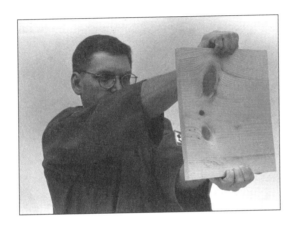

This kind of breaking uses 1 x 12 white pine boards in 10-inch or 12-inch pieces. Thicker boards, harder kinds of wood, cinder and concrete slabs, and other items are used in demonstrations and at more advanced levels of breaking.

ry purpose of this kind of board-breaking is to develop confidence in your techniques and combinations–to prove to yourself that your Taekwondo techniques will work for you in competition and in self-defense without injuring yourself as a result of executing them.

Adults can break at the white-belt level. Regular training in breaking is not recommended for most children because their bones are still growing, and breaking regularly could be traumatic. However, advanced children–those who have been training for a year or more–do occasionally break boards for demonstrations and promotional testing.

Before you practice breaking, make sure you are executing strikes properly. Don't use breaking to learn techniques. Practice breaking to test what you've learned.

This kind of breaking uses 1 x 12 white pine boards in 10-inch or 12-inch pieces. Thicker boards, harder kinds of wood, cinder and concrete slabs, and other items are used in demonstrations and at more advanced levels of break-

Spacers (arrows), such as dominoes or pencils, placed between boards make breaking a little easier than placing two boards flush against each other, but breaking two boards with spacers is still more difficult than breaking just one board.

ing. Spacers placed between boards make breaking a little easier than placing two boards flush against each other, but breaking two boards with spacers is still more difficult than breaking just one board.

The ability to break one board is all that's necessary to show that a technique will work in competition and in self-defense. Breaking a human bone requires about as much pressure as it takes to break one 1 x 12 x 12 pine board.

Without training, any adult man or woman could probably break one board. In fact, breaking with brute force, throwing yourself at the target, you might be able to muscle your way through two or three boards. Still, this doesn't mean you can be effective in self-defense or in competition with that technique. In self-defense situations and in competition you must be well balanced, quick, and powerful, you must strike the target precisely, and you must retract the weapon (arm or leg) quickly to be able to defend or strike again.

Proper training lets you advance through levels of breaking in which you demonstrate this effectiveness in increasingly more complicated circumstances.

Three Basic Breaks

Without more advanced methods of conditioning, the weapons used in this kind of breaking are non-bony—the palm-heel, knife-hand, and ball of the foot. The only conditioning required with these weapons is the conditioning of your normal class training, including work with kicking shields, focus pads, and a heavy bag.

Holding

Holding boards for someone who is breaking is a vital skill. Keep the thumbs and fingers tucked. Have as little of your hand on the board as possible.

Hold the board along the middle sides as shown so that the surfaces of the board are clamped between your fingertips *(right arrow)* and the fat part of the base of your palm. Place your thumb *(left arrow)* at the edge of the board and keep the thumb parallel to that edge. Make sure the wood is aligned so the break occurs with the grain.

Holding one board with two people is best because two people can support the board better than one person.

With one board, if the holder retracts, there is a good chance the board will not break. However, if the technique is executed correctly, the holder shouldn't have enough time to retract. Retraction occurs when the breaker drives into the person or is off center on the strike.

Communication between breaker and holder is also important. Be certain always to establish clear signals.

The mechanics of each of these breaks is the same. They are explained fully for the right-hand palm heel.

• **Right-hand palm heel.** Position yourself in an extended front stance, having your left foot forward, a little longer than usual, with your left leg just beyond the board. Align the right leg with the center of the target. The left hand extends and touches the target first. Retract your left arm into chamber, extending your right arm to the target. Exhale when you touch the board with the breaking hand. On the third touch, execute a strong *kihap*, retract strongly, and twist your hips and shoulders toward the target, striking the center of the board.

Imagine seeing a person's chest six to 12 inches beyond the target. Your palm-heel is not actually going as far as that, but you are imagining it in this way because your focus—the proper mind set–is beyond the board.

At the point of contact, you start retracting, but you do not just touch the target and pull back. You drive your palm heel into the target. When you are into the target, then you pull back. This technique is like driving your palm-heel into a large bowl of jelly. When you are *into it*–not through it–you pull back. You should understand how this focus is different from envisioning going "through" the target.

• **Right knife-hand strike.** Position yourself the same as you would for the right-hand palm heel strike. Imagine striking an attacker's nose or face. The palm faces upward to execute this knife-hand strike.

• **Right front snap kick.** Place the target so that when you strike it, your leg extends about halfway. This means you want to line up on the target a little farther from the target than you would in the previous two hand breaks.

Right-hand palm-heel break. At the point of contact, you start retracting, but you don't just touch the target and pull back. You drive your palm heel into the target. When you're into the target, pull back. This technique is like driving your palm heel into a large bowl of jelly. When you're *into it*—not through it—you pull back. This focus is different from envisioning going "through" the target.

The right knife-hand strike. Position yourself just the same as you would for the right-hand palm-heel strike. Imagine striking an attacker's nose or face. The palm faces upward to execute this knife-hand strike.

Right front snap kick. Place the target so that when you strike it, your leg extends about halfway. This means you want to line up on the target a little farther from the target than you would in the previous two hand breaks.

Advancing

Start with one-station breaking. This means breaking one board with one of the above techniques. You position yourself in front of the board, concentrating on body positioning, breathing, focus, and technique.

When you can break effectively at one station, move to two stations. A two-station break might include someone holding a board in front of you and someone holding another board on your right. You break the first board in front of you with a palm-heel strike and the board on your right with a front snap kick, for example.

The specific strikes don't matter as much as your ability to break the boards while you maintain speed, focus, balance, and recovery. You want to work toward performing these breaks without counting, special breathing exercises, or other preparations you might go through when you practice one-station breaking.

You progress from one-station and two-station breaking to multi-station breaks, turning with each station in different directions with different techniques. You can also increase the level of difficulty by breaking two boards at each station. Generally speaking, the ability to break two boards at five stations showing proper stances, execution, power, speed, retraction, recovery, and breathing demonstrates a high level of effectiveness.

This training simulates your ability to defend yourself against one, two, or more attackers, depending on how many stations you incorporate.

Thus, breaking is one way you can confirm that your class kicking and punching drills will actually work in competition and in self-defense.

Breaking with Blocks

Most students think of breaking as a test of offensive srikes, such as power-kicks and punches.

Breaking is also useful for testing the effectiveness of blocks. If you execute a block correctly, like this outside–inside forearm block, you should be able to break a board with it. If your block can shatter a board, think what your block will be able to do to a weapon coming at you!

Forearm blocks, low blocks, knife-hand blocks, and high blocks are candidates to test with breaking.

A side kick break. The specific strikes don't matter as much as your ability to break the boards while you maintain speed, focus, balance, and recovery. You want to work toward performing these breaks without counting, special breathing exercises, or other preparations you might go through when you practice one-station breaking.

21. Seminar Smarts

Sixteen Ways to Get the Most Out of Martial Arts Seminars

ATTENDING a martial arts seminar is a great way to delve deeply into a specific aspect of Taekwondo training, get acquainted with an unfamiliar martial-arts style, or explore a related subject. A seminar can provide a change of pace for your training, and a seminar is a good place to meet other martial artists.

Let these 16 ideas help you get the most from the experience.

1. **Bring a notebook** and pencil. Take notes, but don't just write down only what the seminar presenter says. Write also how you will apply the information in your Taekwondo training. In this way your notes will become more than just an accumulation of information—they can help you implement these new ideas that you hear.

Take notes, but don't just write down only what the seminar presenter says. Write also how you'll apply the information in your Taekwondo training. In this way your notes become more than just an accumulation of information—they can help you implement the new ideas you hear.

Take full advantage of question-and-answer periods (below) by jotting down questions as you think of them.

2. **Watch for the "big idea."**
   Some seminar regulars say that at any time during a seminar they may suddenly think of a pivotal idea, a monumental thought or application. They say that what they learn from a seminar's "big idea," or several "big ideas," is often worth the cost of the entire seminar.

Be sure to write down your thoughts at such a critical moment so that you don't forget a "big idea" as the presentation moves on.

3. **During a seminar,** take full advantage of question-and-answer periods by jotting down questions as you think of them.

4. **Keep an open mind during** a presentation and be receptive to new ideas. Seminars disappoint some Taekwondo practitioners because they expect only confirmation and reinforcement for their current ideas and practices. They do get that, but what they also get is a flood of new approaches and techniques. Let seminars enrich your Taekwondo training and broaden your experience. Be ready for the unexpected.

5. **Take advantage of advance registration,** if available. If you attend several seminars each year, the money you save on advance registration, compared with the cost of registering at the door, could pay for an entire extra seminar. Furthermore, at some seminars those who have registered in advance avoid lines at the door. Sometimes advance registration lets you take advantage of special rates at local motels. Inquire about special room rates for seminar participants when you register.

6. **Before a session, talk to martial artists** who have attended a seminar offered by the same seminar leader. Ask what you might expect. Will the seminar be more physically demanding, or will it be more "sit-down"? Should you wear your uniform? What equipment will you need, and what equipment, if any, will be provided?

In seminars that focus on technique, the instructor will probably demonstrate a technique and ask participants to pair off. Pick a partner at your level of training or someone who's a little more advanced than you are.

7. **If you plan to attend a weapons seminar** and you are unfamiliar with the weapons, you might want to obtain them before the seminar. In this way you can at least handle the weapons somewhat and become comfortable holding them.

8. **Make sure a seminar you plan to attend** is geared to your level. If you're a beginner, don't go to a seminar at which only advanced techniques are taught, because you'll get little out of the presentation. Furthermore, the risk of injury increases if you train at a much more advanced skill level than your current level.

9. **In seminars that focus on technique,** the instructor will probably demonstrate a technique and ask participants to pair off. Pick a partner at your level of training or someone who's a little more advanced than you are.

10. **The seminar leader and the assistants** usually check participants as they practice. Take notes during these practice periods and write down the constructive ideas you hear.

11. **Practice the techniques** as much as you can while you're at the seminar. If the seminar spans two or more days, review the day's content each evening. It is also important to make time at home to practice techniques you learn during a seminar.

12. **Bring training accessories with you** to ensure your comfort. Remember that seminars are different from classes. Most presentations last a full day or several days, and seminars are often whirlwinds of training—fast-paced events that are crammed with ideas, techniques, and practice.

If you attend a seminar that's going to be physically demanding, prepare for prolonged, strenuous activity. Bring a water bottle and sip lightly during long, vigorous training periods. Bring a towel or two. Don't eat a big meal before a seminar in which you'll be training hard. Eat lightly during physically demanding seminars.

13. **Before a physically demanding seminar,** rest adequately. Arrive early so that you can warm up and stretch. Get enough rest during the seminar, especially during seminars that last days. Replenish yourself. Don't just collapse in your motel room after the day's activities. Cool down and stretch after each workout.

14. **If you plan to attend an outdoor seminar,** or if a portion of a seminar will be outdoors, bring sunblock and insect repellent in case you need them.

15. **Seek out complementary sources of information** on seminar subjects. As a Taekwondo practitioner you know that repetition is basic to learning. Long after the seminar, reading books and viewing tapes on the seminar's content can help bolster the ideas you learn.

Furthermore, the seminar presenter might offer books and tapes on the subject, along with training aids and equipment. The presenter might also recommend sources with which you might not be familiar. Bring money so that you can purchase these items at the seminar. Even though you probably can take order forms home with you, seminar presenters sometimes offer discounts to participants on books, tapes, and equipment.

16. **Watch for informal, unannounced activities,** and get in on them. During a break at a two-day seminar, two instructors compared and demonstrated take-downs, discussing the effectiveness of each technique and the differences between their styles.

After the Seminar

To make the most of a seminar, act on your ideas. Researchers know that if seminar participants don't apply new ideas they have learned within one day, the participants often forget the ideas. Before you leave the seminar, while the new information is fresh, take a few minutes to write down several specific ways you can apply the seminar content within the next 24 hours. When you arrive home, write a letter to someone or to yourself on how you can apply what you have learned. Outline a training plan that incorporates the most vital new ideas you learned. Phone a friend and describe a plan of action. Tape-record your ideas on putting the new know-how to work.

Remember—whatever you do after a seminar, before that 24-hour period passes apply the new ideas you learned.

Several seminar participants gathered around the instructors and took part in this impromptu "mini-class." These students said that they learned more about take-downs in 20 minutes than they had learned in weeks of training.

22. Rest

A̶RE YOU TRAINING too hard, greatly increasing your risk of injury? Are you not training hard enough, thereby lessening the benefits of training?

"Unfortunately, determining how far to push yourself and how much rest you need takes much trial and error," says Dr. Mark Mascari, a Harrisburg, Pennsylvania-based physician and Taekwondo practitioner. "It's a matter of learning through continued training what your body can and cannot do, and figuring out when to rest more and when to train harder."

Mascari says that most people don't like pain and discomfort, so they don't push themselves to achieve what they could. If these people could be encouraged to push just a little each time they train, they could better learn what their limitations are.

Unfortunately, determining how far to push yourself and how much rest you need takes much trial and error. It's a matter of learning through continued training what your body can and cannot do, and figuring out when to rest more and when to train harder.

Most people don't like pain and discomfort, so they don't push themselves to achieve what they could. If these people could be encouraged to push just a little each time they train, they could better learn their limitations. Physical ability, current level of conditioning, and age are some of the factors that each of us must consider.

"In Taekwondo training, not every pain is a bad pain, but, in general, pain is nature's way of telling you to stop," Mascari points out. "Like anything in life, in Taekwondo training if you don't try, you'll never learn your limits."

Identifying specific do's and don'ts is an individual, continuing pursuit. So understanding what rest is and how the body works can help you set reasonable limits.

The Basics of Rest

Mascari says that rest has little to do with the body's soft tissues—muscles, tendons, and ligaments—or the hard tissues, the bones. "Rest deals more with the central nervous system, and re-regulating the central nervous system, most often through sleep. Rest involves the nerves that bring messages to the muscles, which is different from muscle wear and tear. The rest that sore or injured soft tissues need is inactivity, which gives the soft tissues time to heal. Adequate rest most often means improving or normalizing the nervous system."

Mascari says that people deprived of sleep become neurologically dysfunctional—the thought processes slow and the hands jitter, for example. Similarly, if you're extremely tired and you continue to train, the lack of rest makes your Taekwondo slow, sloppy, and less accurate. You are then more likely to make a mistake that could cause an injury.

This lack of rest is not a factor in muscle wear and tear. Muscle fatigue is caused by exercising beyond a muscle's oxygen and nutritional capacity. Muscles contract by way of myofibrils—the cellular level of a muscle. Electrical impulses from the brain induce the myofibrils to contract by sliding over one another.

The blood supply carries oxygen and nutrition (glucose) that allow the muscle to contract. If you require a muscle to contract faster than you can supply it with blood, that muscle will use its own oxygen supply; but muscles can't store oxygen efficiently, so they deplete that supply quickly.

Repetitions and speed of muscle contraction exhaust a muscle's capacity. When the muscle contracts, it also pinches off its own blood supply. Forced contractions can impede blood flow to replenish the muscle to do more work.

As you force the muscle to contract in an anaerobic condition (no oxygen), the muscle quickly builds lactic acid. Lactic acid is a byproduct of anaerobic activity. That's the "burn" you feel in the muscles during a workout. It occurs when you've exhausted your oxygen supply and you require the muscle still to work. Lactic acid causes pain—it burns the area as any acid would burn the skin, for example. Working beyond this point could damage your muscles even more.

If you haven't worked out in a while, if you're out of shape, or if you are relatively new to Taekwondo, the body has not adjusted to the extra requirements of training. When you require the body to provide more oxygen and nutrients than it's capable of supplying, you create an anaerobic condition, which builds lactic acid. Lactic acid causes the pH of the blood to drop, which contributes to causing damage to all the body's soft tissue—muscles, ligaments, and tendons. Remember that progress in training is slow and steady.

Can you build your capacity by working through this pain? "To some extent, but you also damage the muscles," says Mascari. "If you follow the idea of 'no pain, no gain' beyond this point long enough, you cause irreparable damage in scar tissue formation, which takes the flexibility out of a muscle and defeats your long-term Taekwondo training goals."

When you take a muscle to failure, as you might in weight training (see Chapter 4), you're trying to change the muscle environmentally. This means that in time and with appropriate rest between workouts, the body will lay down more muscle cells to perform the extra work, and use the body's energy sources more efficiently.

"Many people take this training to a point at which they damage themselves," Mascari points out. "Taking muscles to total failure increases the chances of causing irreparable damage to the muscles. The thinking is that taking a muscle to total failure requires each myofibril muscle cell to work, so you're getting the maximum amount of muscle working toward your maximum capacity of conditioning. If you use less weight and fewer repetitions, you use less muscle to accomplish the task.

"The muscles do regenerate and grow back stronger, but rest is vital to this rebuilding and repairing. Resting helps the body bring nutrition to the area so that the damage is allowed to heal."

Danger Signs

Frequent yawning can be a sign that you need to rest. It's a physical request for oxygen, and it could be a sign of fatigue. A general lack of focus can also mean you need to rest. Part of a general lack of focus could also include sustaining injuries you never had before. Muscle fatigue isn't usually the culprit here. The central nervous system—nerves that send the messages to the muscles—needs to be re-regulated with appropriate rest and sleep.

"Muscle cramps could suggest the need for rest. However, there is no direct physiological relationship between cramping and fatigue," Mascari says. "Muscle cramps are usually a sign of dehydration, and dehydration could suggest overtraining. A muscle goes into static contraction—a cramp—when it's not supplied with enough blood, oxygen and nutrients. If you exercise too much, you might sweat profusely, which can dehydrate you and cause a cramp."

Rest and Stretching

When you sustain an injury, you have to rest to prevent further injury to the area. "When you sustain an injury, the body protects itself with scar tissue," Mascari says. "Scar tissue is less flexible and less durable than normal connective tissue. It's always prone to more injury. Once you become injured, resting helps prevent further injury and allows the body to heal. But the injured area will never be as good as it was before."

Mascari explains that when a ligament is stretched out of shape, the body creates scar tissue so that it's not as loose. When you break a bone, the body lays down calcium around the break. When you injure a muscle by stretching it too much or by contracting it too much, scar tissue replaces the injured muscle tissue, and you'll be less flexible there. These responses to injury are the body's way of protecting itself from further injury.

If you don't stretch and make the normal muscle on both sides of the injured area com-

pensate for strength and flexibility, you'll lose flexibility in total. Suppose a muscle is five inches long, and you injure a half-inch of the muscle by over-stretching. The body replaces the damaged muscle tissue with scar tissue, which is not flexible. Now the stretchable portion of the muscle is four inches. To regain the same stretch you achieved with the original five inches of muscle, you must stretch and strengthen both sides of the muscle to compensate for the half-inch loss.

"With most injuries to soft tissue, it's best to let the injuries heal and let the scar tissue do what's it's going to do," Mascari suggests. "Then you compensate with stretching and strengthening. The worst thing to do is return to training too hard and too fast. Then you never let scar tissue form, and the injured area will be an area of weakness forever. The best strategy when you're injured is to compensate to regain flexibility and tone after the injury has had sufficient time to heal."

Rest and Conditioning

If you haven't worked out in a while, if you're out of shape, or if you're relatively new to Taekwondo training, the body hasn't adjusted to the extra requirements of training. You'll also have a lack of flexibility in the ligaments and tendons. When you require the body to provide more oxygen and nutrients than it is capable of supplying, you create an anaerobic condition, which builds lactic acid. Lactic acid causes the pH of the blood to drop, which contributes to causing damage to all the body's soft tissue—muscles, ligaments, and tendons.

For this reason, rest is vital to give the muscles a chance to rebuild.

Progress in conditioning is slow in Taekwondo training. You often don't see the gains you make until you stop training for one reason or another, but improved conditioning does appear on many levels. As your conditioning improves, you will notice an increase in your capacity—your body will better exchange oxygen from the air to the lungs and bloodstream, and to the muscles, tendons, and ligaments that require it. Your ability to inhale will increase by expanding your lungs. This enhances your ability to use oxygen. Your blood vessels will dilate, which drops blood pressure. Dilation of the blood vessels also relaxes the blood vessels so that your heart doesn't have to work as hard. You'll experience improved blood flow. This means that more nutrients can go to the limbs and torso for more work, whereas before, the lungs and heart required the oxygen and nutrients, thus causing your arms and legs to fatigue faster.

Increased blood flow and its accompanying surge of nutrients and oxygen also reduce the amount of lactic acid that your body will produce. You'll fatigue less because in a field of oxygen all your muscles work better. The rapid breathing that occurs when you're not conditioned well is your body's reaction to a lack of oxygen. This is called hypoxia: the need for oxygen and a lack of oxygen in the bloodstream. Conditioning lets you use oxygen much better. You use less oxygen to do the same tasks that previously may have winded you.

All in all, remember that over a long time you have to find your own training limits through trial and error. This period includes mostly your unranked years. In Taekwondo, earning a black belt means, partly, that you've learned the basic techniques. It also means that you've begun to know your body's limitations—when to push yourself and when to rest.

The process is continual because our capacities change. Thus, a large part of learning how to train at any level of skill is understanding how your body reacts to training, taking care of yourself to minimize injuries, and letting yourself heal properly when you are injured. This is the process that lets you benefit the most from Taekwondo training.

Training to Rest During Competition

Conditioning and recovery time are keys to success in full-contact fighting and Olympic-style Taekwondo. In round competition, you're most often given one minute between rounds. In open tournaments, you have a similar brief period to rest.

Learning to rest *briefly in competition is vital because you must prepare your body for periods of total exertion during one-minute or two-minute rounds and then rest for a minute. The key is to learn to recuperate by working on your recovery time.*

Continuing to spar in rounds—just doing what you're training for—is appropriate training. You could also jump rope. Another effective training regimen includes 40-yard wind sprints with a walk-back to simulate recovery time. In this training, you'd take about one minute to walk back to the starting point—about the same time you're allowed for recovery between rounds. When you reach the starting point, sprint again. During your rest periods, remember to control your breathing—providing your body with as much oxygen as you can. You must also keep moving by walking. During these rest periods don't sit or lie down.

23. When "Indomitable Spirit" Hits Home

Overcoming Obstacles Makes the Meaning of "Indomitable Spirit" Clear

SEVERAL MONTHS AFTER I BEGAN Taekwondo training, something happened to me during one class that I'll never forget. The class was about to perform horse-stance punching. I let out a *kihap*, lowered myself into a horse stance, and began punching. But this time the horse stance and my punching felt different from before. In the horse stance I suddenly felt as if I were bolted to the center of the earth. My toes tingled. The instructor's occasional attempt to sweep my feet and upset my balance didn't work.

I also could feel that I was no longer over-extending as I punched. I had "found my distance." I wasn't straining, either, and I could feel how much more powerful my punches were. The knuckles of my index and middle fingers felt glowingly warm.

Suddenly the horse-stance punching finally felt "right" after months of just going through the motions. In that instant, that one lesson settled in me at last. In a flash I understood and I made the technique mine.

What a special moment that was–the instant my technique inched to a higher level. My mind

The training path isn't always easy and smooth. *When the going gets tough, adopting the idea of "indomitable spirit" reinforces one's perseverance. That's a "must" in Taekwondo training.*

raced for days after that class. Possibilities that I had previously believed I could not attain suddenly seemed reachable.

I had begun Taekwondo training at age 40 because for more than 20 years I had always wanted to practice a martial art but never made the time for it. I also wanted to reap the benefits of an exercise program and lose 40 pounds. Now I was progressing quite noticeably. And during my first six months of training I had lost and held off nearly 30 pounds. "This is easy," I thought.

For some time after this experience I settled into a rhythm as I trained, climbing to similar peaks, separated by months of waiting on plateaus. I tolerated the plateaus as I trained, because I saw that sooner or later I would leap to the next height.

I began to practice specifically to experience those training summits. I anticipated the thrill of climbing onto the next plateau, as I did when the horse-stance punching suddenly "clicked" for me. The weight stayed off, too. I continued to convince myself how easy martial-arts training was.

Don't let setbacks stop your training. *If you sustain an injury that keeps you from regular classroom training, rehearse your forms and other techniques in your mind. Walk through forms and techniques. You can always regain losses in conditioning.*

"You strained a groin muscle," the doctor said. "Sometimes in these cases people actually pull off pieces of the pelvic bone. It appears you didn't do that. You're lucky."

I quivered. "There's still a lot I can do in class," I said.

"No, no," he said. "You're 40 years old, not 18. I'm just thinking about your health. No kicking. No running. Not even brisk walking. You need to rest that leg. Stay off the leg until the pain goes away completely–plus two weeks more."

The doctor saw my disappointment. "Look," he said, "if you do return to Taekwondo training, you should make some adjustments. Some people can train five, six times a week. You can't, at least not now."

Feeling Defeated

I felt beaten up, even though I knew my condition could have been much worse and that other martial artists have overcome considerably more than a groin pull. Still, I knew that this injury was serious and that the doctor was right.

I spent that summer away from class, brooding and complaining. Almost every day, though, I walked through and rehearsed all the forms and techniques I knew. Day after day I wondered if the combination of my age, physical ability, and injury meant that my martial-arts training had actually ended. "Who's kidding who?" I asked myself. "Should I quit? Could my Taekwondo training end as quickly as I began to notice my own progress?"

Eight weeks later the doctor said, "OK, you can get on with it, but go slowly. If you feel pain, stop." I began walking briskly at first and stretching lightly. I still feared that my training was over and that I was just fooling myself. A few weeks later, still worried, I returned to Taekwondo class and began practicing again–slowly and lightly.

I understood then how individual training actually is. That groin strain was a gentle tap on the shoulder reminding me that my 40-year-old body would progress at my pace–no one else's.

During this period, several students and I were chatting with one of the instructors after class. At that time we were engaging in the predictable inquiries of how long one has trained and when one received each belt.

The instructor told us how long he had been training and briefly recounted his martial-arts biography. Then he paused and said, "Listen, you guys. My teacher told me something that has always stuck with me and I want to tell you the same thing. He said, 'If you want a black belt, take mine. If you want to *earn* a black belt, take patience.' "

I dismissed those words quickly. I understood, but I could not embrace their meaning. I didn't know how deeply they would soon affect me. My training so far seemed easy and I believed I was invincible. My limited experience suggested that nothing in martial-arts training could disappoint me.

I was wrong. When I was a green belt, after class one evening I felt a dull ache at the top of my inner left thigh. Sometimes the pain burned a little, sometimes it ached more, sometimes it was gone. This on-and-off dull pain lasted for more than a month, and I finally had my doctor check it out.

Taking "indomitable spirit" from the training hall to the schoolroom helps students get better grades. It focuses their attention on appropriate influences and enhances achievement in all areas. This idea works in school, at work, in personal relationships, in the family—everywhere.

Sure, I would love to be in my teens or twenties again. I wish I had been in better physical condition all along. Nevertheless, I knew that the price of crossing that realistic training line a few more times could be much higher.

Slammed Spirits

Then, after only a few weeks of training, another injury slammed my spirits again—my lower back this time. Once more the doctor told me how lucky I was. "Just simple back pain," he said, "the result of neglect over the years and weak abdominals. You're not 18, you know. Set a more realistic pace for yourself or you're going to pay dearly."

Again I couldn't go to Taekwondo class—this time a month. I pouted some more and continued to complain. During this period I concentrated on stretching, strengthening and relaxing my back, and I reverted to my familiar routine of walking through techniques.

Many times I closed my eyes and imagined I was in class. I saw the faces of the students, heard the occasional ring of the office telephone, recalled the fresh-paint-like smell of the training area, felt my uniform around me and

the headband and wristband I usually wear, and heard my instructors' voices. Then, with my eyes still closed, I rehearsed techniques.

Bolted to the Center of the Earth

I returned to class again, easing back into the training. Several weeks later my teacher called me to the front of the class and asked me to perform a form. When I began, I suddenly felt that my blocks, punches, and kicks were stronger than ever before. My stances felt solid and comfortable, and I re-experienced that sensation of being bolted to the center of the earth as I locked into each stance.

The same feeling that once exhilarated me during horse-stance punching overtook me, and again I unexpectedly climbed onto another training summit. All that quiet drilling and walking through forms and techniques paid off. While I was injured both times, I had been rehearsing—a common method used in the martial arts and in many other endeavors to sharpen focus and improve performance.

"Take patience" indeed. That summer I learned a special meaning for the idea of "indomitable spirit"—a lesson on patience. I had faced two setbacks and reshaped them into lasting benefits. I refashioned them unknowingly, but I reshaped them nonetheless.

I now know my body much better than before. After years of neglect, I take care of my back with regular stretching, strengthening, and relaxing. I am also careful not to stretch that groin muscle beyond its limit. I know that I can go as far as I want in my training, but to do so I have to adjust the pace.

Savoring Each Class

My training is by no means over–the pace is just slower and more deliberate. Now I joyfully train two, maybe three times a week. What I gave up in quantity I've gained in quality. I savor each class and dwell on each tidbit of knowledge I learn. What I gave up in frequency of training I've gained in longevity of training. As long as I am physically capable and as long as other personal and family matters permit it, I'll simply continue to train.

You might think that the idea of "indomitable spirit" entails mostly suffering, struggle, and conflict. Sometimes it might. But the benefit of embracing the idea is incalculable.

Letting "indomitable spirit" work for you is like climbing a mountain. Going up is difficult, and it might seem as if it's always going to be that way, until you reach the top. Then you look down all around you. You take a breather, re-evaluate your circumstances, and gain a fresh perspective. That's when you can make the best, most constructive decisions.

The fact is, Taekwondo training satisfies me now more than before. Those training plateaus and peaks are still there, only now I don't anticipate them. I just acknowledge and appreciate them when I recognize their occurrence. They've become part of a larger idea of plateaus and peaks and progress–self-improvement not only in Taekwondo class but in all aspects of my life.

Sometimes students embrace the idea of "indomitable spirit" without knowing it as such. Either way, winning is winning.

Trying to Help

When students tell me their difficulties and that they're thinking of quitting, I tell them my story. My experience may not be as heart-wrenching as are the ordeals of some Taekwondo practitioners, but the lesson is the same–in and out of class. When the opportunity arises, I try to help fellow students, business associates, and my family–especially my children–make it up their own mountains, high enough so they can look down on a problem, see it differently from before, and consider solutions and options they might otherwise overlook.

Of course a setback in training or in anything else is disappointing. Of course you have to work doubly hard to overcome difficulties. Of course you have to keep trying and trying and trying.

That's the point. The idea of "indomitable spirit" is a process in which you sometimes take one step backward to move two steps ahead.

About the Authors

Master Joe Fox holds a 5th Degree Black Belt in Taekwondo and a 7th Degree Black Belt in American Karate. He has been teaching Taekwondo for some twenty years. He is head instructor and president/owner of the Harrisburg Institute of Taekwondo, in Harrisburg, Pennsylvania.

Art Michaels is an award-winning editor, writer, and photographer. He has published more than 600 articles and some 1000 photographs in a great variety of magazines and books. He holds a 1st Degree Black Belt in Taekwondo.

Index